What Jesus Asks

What Jesus Asks
Meditations on Questions in the Gospels

by Harry B. Adams

CBP Press
St. Louis, Missouri

© Copyright 1986 CBP Press

All rights reserved. No part of this book may be reproduced by any method without the publisher's written permission. Address:

CBP Press
Box 179
St. Louis, MO 63166

All scripture quotations, unless otherwise indicated, are from the Revised Standard Version of the Bible, copyrighted 1946, 1952, © 1971, 1973 by the Division of Christian Education of the National Council of Churches of Christ in the United States of America, and used by permission.

Library of Congress Cataloging-in-Publication Data

Adams, Harry Baker, 1924-
    What Jesus Asks.

    Includes index.
    1. Jesus Christ—Words—Meditations.   I. Title.
BT306.A33   1986   232.9'54   85-18991
ISBN 0-8272-4217-4

Printed in the United States of America

Contents

High Praise for This Book

"Dean Adams deals with Jesus' questions as if they were addressed to Christians today in so simple and direct a fashion as to require answers. Those answers betray who we are and where we are going. To ponder his questions and our answers should, therefore, be of great benefit to many readers."

—Paul Minear

"I found this a refreshingly original approach to the fascinating theme of Jesus' questions. It is delightful to find a biblical study that is very well written and avoids the cliches of much popular homiletics. It speaks very directly to the intelligent believer or unbeliever, and I wish it well."

—David H. C. Read

"In every case, Harry has treated those questions honestly and fairly, responding in ways that are clear, helpful, and very practical. He has, however, held his comments always under the discipline and judgment of the gospel . . . not offering just good advice, but spelling out the meaning of the gospel in some of the major arenas of a person's life."

—Fred B. Craddock

Introduction

"Jesus answered them, 'I also will ask you a question'" (Matt. 21:24).

Every politician has to learn how to answer questions, and must learn how not to answer questions while appearing to do so. That politician has to give the impression that he deals honestly, forthrightly, and wisely with every question put forth.

The candidate will have a different problem depending on the kind of question being dealt with. Some questions can be answered boldly, openly, and emphatically. Do you believe in motherhood and the American way of life? Some questions are obviously designed to trap the candidate. Have you stopped lying to the American people? Some questions will get the candidate in trouble, no matter what the answer, because there are sharply conflicting positions on abortion, or prayer in public school, or support for Israel. Some questions raise issues so complex and subtle that no three-sentence answer can deal with them.

From time to time in his ministry, Jesus had to face questions about who he was and what he was doing. "And when he entered the temple, the chief priests and the elders of the people came up to him as he was teaching and said, 'By what authority are you doing these things, and who gave you this authority?'" (Matt. 21:23). Many of us would like to put that question to Jesus, along with some other questions. Just exactly who are you? What precisely do you want me to do? What is God like, and what is your relationship to God? Why are there evil and suffering in the world? How did the world begin and how will it end? What is life after death like?

Jesus didn't answer the question of the chief priests and the elders about his authority. Why not? The scripture doesn't say, but it's not too difficult to figure out why he declined to answer. It wasn't an honest question. Even if Jesus had defined his authority, his questioners weren't about to accept it, no matter what he said. It was a question designed to trap him. Whatever answer Jesus gave, they would try to turn it against him. If he said that his authority was from God, they would accuse him of blasphemy. If he said his authority was from any other source, they would say that he had no right to do what he was doing. Furthermore, it was a question that didn't permit an easy answer. It took a lifetime of working and living for Jesus to manifest what God was doing in and through him.

So Jesus didn't answer the question. Rather he asked a question of his own. "Jesus answered them, 'I also will ask you a question; and if you tell me the answer, then I also will tell you by what authority I do these things. The baptism of John, whence was it? From heaven or from men?'" (Matt. 21:24f.). They had tried to make things difficult for Jesus with their question. Jesus refused to be trapped, and instead asked them a question that put them in a dilemma. "And they argued with one another, 'If we say, "from heaven," he will say to us, "Why then did you not believe him?" But if we say, "From men," we are afraid of the multitude; for all hold that John was a prophet'" (Matt. 21:25f.).

The incident reveals the skillful use that Jesus made of questions. We have a lot of questions we would like to put to Jesus if we had the chance, but in fact it is Jesus who puts the questions to us. In the Gospel accounts of the teaching and ministry of Jesus, there are recorded over 150 questions that Jesus put to the people who came to him. Jesus expresses the reality that God is not the one to answer our questions, but the one who puts questions to us. In thinking about the questions we would like to ask Jesus, we must acknowledge that often we don't know how to ask appropriately. We ask questions out of idle curiosity, questions that serve our self-interests, questions that push beyond the limits of human finitude. As we ask, it comes clear that we are still tempted to try to be like God in what we know.

But as we encounter God in Jesus Christ, he asks us the questions. In confronting the people with whom he dealt, Jesus put questions to probe what they were doing, questions to help them face who they were and what they were about. As we enter into relationship with Jesus Christ, we don't come to ask him questions, to force him to explain himself, to have all our confusions clarified and all our mysteries solved.

In these meditations we face some of the questions that Jesus asked the people who came to him, and that he continues to ask us as we come to him. It is typical of Jesus to say, "I also will ask you a question." He asks not in idle curiosity, nor to trap us, nor to press us to give "the right answer." He puts the questions to us to help us discern who we are, where we are going, and what we most truly believe.

1

What Credit Is That to You?

The Question of Jesus
"If you love those who love you, what credit is that to you? . . .
And if you do good to those who do good to you, what credit is
that to you? . . . And if you lend to those from whom you hope to
receive, what credit is that to you?" (Luke 6:32-34).

As a couple approached the door of a hotel where a reception
was being given, one of them turned to the spouse and asked,
"How long do we have to stay at this affair?" It's the kind of
question asked in many circumstances. What is the minimum?
What is the least we can get away with? The couple going to the
reception are under some kind of social obligation to attend the
affair, but are eager to get out as soon as they can decently do so
without offending their host or the guest of honor. They calculate
carefully how little they can safely invest in this occasion.

There are many occasions that prompt people to find the
minimum expected of them. A teacher gives an assignment, and
the first question inevitably will be: "How long does it have to
be? How many pages do we have to write?" A young person
taking piano lessons wants to know how much time has to be
spent practicing and watches the clock with care so that not a
minute too much will be invested. As the solicitor for the church
or the heart fund or whatever stands at the door, there is quick
calculation of what the smallest acceptable gift can be.

All of us deal with some situations by asking what is the
minimum demanded of us. The demand may come from those

who have some kind of authority over us, and we want to know what is the least we can do to satisfy that authority. The demand may come from our own sense of what would be socially acceptable, and we seek the least we can do without risking embarrassment of loss of face. We all live under legal demands, the demand to pay taxes for example, and we certainly don't want to pay more than is absolutely required.

Another way we deal with the obligations of life is to get all the conditions straight before we venture into an agreement or a relationship or a project. Before taking a job a new employee wants to know precisely what the responsibilities of the job are, what hours are to be worked, what wages and fringe benefits are to be paid, how much vacation time is to be allowed, what retirement benefits will be accrued. A student matriculating in a college searches the catalog to find out exactly how many and what courses have to be taken in order to earn the degree. A contractor proposing to add an addition to a house specifies exactly what work will be done, what materials will be used, what the time and method of payment will be. Before agreeing to do something, we want to have all the conditions clear so that there will be no surprises about what is expected of us.

Yet a third way in which we deal with life is to determine in every situation what the profit is for us. The question is pressed about the benefit that will come to us from an investment of time, or from entering a relationship, or from undertaking a project. So there is discussion about the "payoff" of a college degree. A person invited to join a civic club calculates what such membership will mean for business contacts.

Responsible judgment can certainly be made that these three ways of dealing with life are appropriate and even necessary. To establish the minimum expectation, to get terms and conditions clear, to be concerned about the benefits that will accrue are ways of struggling toward a kind of justice. They are ways in which people try to keep themselves from being exploited. They are ways in which the legitimate rights of persons can be protected. When conditions are clear and minimum expectations have been established, the probability of friction in human relationships is reduced. So it is quite understandable that persons are concerned about becoming clear on what the minimum expectation is. Long experience has demonstrated the wisdom of getting every conceivable contingency covered in a contract. Every person has legitimate interests, and if the person doesn't protect those inter-

10

ests, no one else will.

But that question of Jesus puts a different perspective on these ways of dealing with life. "If you love those who love you, what credit is that to you? For even sinners love those who love them. And if you do good to those who do good to you, what credit is that to you? For even sinners do the same. And if you lend to those from whom you hope to receive, what credit is that to you? Even sinners lend to sinners, to receive as much again" (Luke 6:32-34). Life on the basis of the minimums, careful calculation of personal benefit, and some concern for justice and equity would lead persons to love those who love them, to do good to those who do good to them, and to lend to those who can be expected to lend to them.

But then Jesus asks: "What credit is that to you?" The question could be answered with the observation that loving those who love us and doing good to those who do good to us ought to be worth some commendation. After all, there are plenty of people who take advantage of those who love them and who do wrong to those who do good to them. There are those who not only refuse to lend to those who can't repay but who do their best to exploit the weak.

The question as Jesus put it, however, makes clear that he is not commending persons who love those who love them or who do good to those who do good to them. He is not condemning them, but he wants to know what kind of credit they think they can expect for such minimal and self-interested behavior. Another translation of this passage by A.R.C. Leaney gives a fresh perspective on what Jesus is asking. "And if you love them that love you, what grace are you showing? . . . For indeed if you do good to those who do good to you, what grace are you showing? . . . And if you lend to those from whom you hope to receive something, what grace are you showing?" What is there of grace in behavior that is motivated only by the need to protect our own interests? What is there of grace in careful calculation of the benefits coming to us? What is there of grace in the intense concern not to do more than is absolutely required of us?

Careful calculation of responsibility and attention to self-interest are legitimate human concerns, in fact necessary concerns in the complexities of human relationships. But Jesus raises the issue of the adequacy of dealing with life only by seeking the minimum or by calculating personal profit. As we consider how we relate to persons and ponder the concerns that we take into

11

account in approaching every situation, the question of Jesus forces us to take a fresh look at what we are doing. "What credit is that to you?" Or what grace are we expressing in the way we go about our living? As we confront that question and as we reflect on the character of the life of Jesus, we come to know that it is simply not enough to assess every situation by asking what the minimum is or by figuring precisely what the profit is.

Expressing the love that Jesus calls us to manifest moves us beyond the careful calculation at which we become so adept. Love doesn't ask about the minimum that has to be done in order to be acceptable. Love that wants the best for the other doesn't make careful appraisal about the least that can be done. In the face of a desperate human need, love doesn't say, "I've done enough for one day."

Nor does love depend on the lovableness of the other. A delightful little four-year-old girl dressed in an immaculate pink dress holds out her arms and wants to be hugged. It doesn't take a great deal of grace to respond to her beauty and affection, and surely it is good to lift her up and give her the affection she seeks. An intoxicated old man with filthy clothes and smelly breath plants himself on the sidewalk beseeching help from all who pass him. He has nothing to offer anyone. It takes a full measure of grace to express love and compassion for a derelict who has probably reached his present sorry state because of his own weaknesses.

Love does not demand that it be reciprocated. Surely love rejoices when it is shared, when the loved one responds with warmth and affection. But there is an unconditional character about love that sets it beyond careful calculation that the other has to love us as much as we love the other. In many families, the time comes when the young assert independence in radical and hurting ways. They reject the values by which their parents have lived. They demand space and distance from the family community. They speak brutal criticism of the ways in which their parents have walked. The hurt is painful, and it is tempting for the parents to lash out in their anger on account of the failed hopes and dreams they had for their children. But there is a staying power in love that perseveres and continues to care, even when the one cared for seems not to care.

"If you love those who love you, what credit is that to you?" Jesus' question pushes us to ask what there has been of grace in our lives. What have we done beyond what we absolutely had to do? It is the giving not demanded of us that expresses grace. What we have done out of concern only for what the blessing will be to another expresses grace. Seeking the welfare of the other expresses grace.

Seeking the minimum, careful stipulation of conditions, and concern for personal profit are pervasive in human affairs. When we look at the way persons actually behave, it is clear that these are the principles that guide the behavior of most folk. Everybody does it this way. But Jesus will not accept the way in which "everybody does it" as sufficient for those who have involved their lives with him. Even sinners love those who love them. Even sinners lend to those who give assurance that they will repay. But that's not good enough for those of us who have made a commitment to the Lord. Jesus Christ asks more of us. When he says, "Love your enemies, and do good, and lend, expecting nothing in return," he is not talking to everybody (Luke 6:35). He is talking to those who have accepted his claim upon them, and who have answered his call to be disciples.

If we simply accept the standards of the world, what credit is that to us, or what grace are we showing? Jesus Christ sets another standard for us. Sinners can love those who love them, but Christ expects us to love those who don't show much love. Sinners can do good to those who do good to them, but Christ expects us to do good to those who do evil. Sinners can offer help to those who will help them in return, but Christ expects us to help those who can never repay what we do for them. If we are ever tempted to take satisfaction in the fact that we do as well as most people do in our dealings with others, the question of Jesus shatters any illusions we may have that doing as well as most people do is sufficient. "What credit is that to you?"

Jesus lays upon us the burden of a heavy commandment. "Love your enemies, and do good, and lend, expecting nothing in return." We do well not to minimize the difficulty of what Jesus is asking of us. Minimum standards attract us. Intense concern for our self-interest shapes our perceptions and our judgments. Loving lovable people seems an attractive way to express what we are called to do. Expecting some return on the love we offer to others strikes us as reasonable. But Jesus doesn't just lay a heavy burden on us. When he calls us to be his kind of person, he offers both promises and resources. "But love your enemies, and do good, and lend, expecting nothing in return." There is the commandment. "And your reward will be great, and you will be sons of the

13

Most High." There is the promise. "For he is kind to the ungrateful and the selfish. Be merciful, even as your Father is merciful" (Luke 6:35f.). There is the resource.

We do not earn our place as children of God by accepting the burden of Jesus' commandments, but we affirm our place before God as we love our enemies and do good to those who can offer us nothing in return. We do not love in order to earn a reward, but there is reward to those who love in the spirit of Christ. Living by minimums and insisting on our profits may seem to be the only reasonable stance to take in our kind of world, where we are always in danger of being used and exploited. But living by minimums stifles the potential of what life can become. To live by minimums is to become a minimum person . The commandment of Christ to move beyond the minimum, loving only those who love us, is an invitation to expand who we are until we truly become those who can be called children of God. There is reward in finding ways to show grace in our living. We may love those who cannot pay us back in the confident assurance that such love enriches our own lives and enables us to become more fully what God intends for us to be. With the commandment to love our enemies, there is the promise that our reward will be great.

With the commandment to love our enemies, there is given the resource to enable us to fulfill what is asked. When we commit ourselves to Jesus Christ as Lord and accept the challenge of living in his way, he offers to us the fullness of the love of God, who "is kind to the ungrateful and selfish." Because we know God's love for us, a love that reaches out to us when we are ungrateful and selfish, we have the possibility of loving even those who have shown no disposition to love us. It is God's love for us that makes possible our love for others.

We are always tempted to adopt the standards of the world around us, to get by with doing as little as possible, to set rigid conditions before making any investment of ourselves, to insure that we will get our fair share in every situation. But that is not the style of life to which Jesus Christ calls us. When we are tempted to limit our love to those who love us, his question prods us: "What credit is that to you?" When we are tempted to do good only to those who do good to us, his question shakes us: "What credit is that to you?" When we are tempted to lend only to those who will do as much for us, his question pushes us: "What credit is that to you?"

2

Who Can Add a Cubit?

The Question of Jesus
"And which of you by being anxious can add a cubit to his span
of life?" (Luke 12:25).

The Connecticut lottery advertises extensively on radio and
television, urging people to purchase tickets for its various games.
One of the features of its daily numbers game that the promoters
pushed at one point was the option of persons to select the
number they wanted. No longer did persons have to take the
number that came up when they bought a ticket, but they could
now pick a particular number. Except for some superstitious
conviction about lucky numbers, it was not entirely clear how
picking one's own number provided any better opportunity for
winning. The odds against winning were still 1000 to 1, and the
payoff was still 500 to 1. But in the ads, the announcer declared
with great excitement that "now you have more control over your
fate."

The notion of fate has a certain ambiguity about it. On the
one hand, to talk about fate is to suggest that a person's destiny is
fixed. Things are ordained by the powers of the universe. In a
rigid view of the notion of fate, all that happens to a person from
the moment of birth to the moment of death is set by forces
outside of the control of the person. The destiny is fixed by the
stars or by some other powers. To accept an interpretation of
human existence that sees it dependent on fate is to believe that
"whatever will be will be."

On the other hand, although the notion of fate has persisted as a way of interpreting human existence, there is deep resistance to the denial of all human freedom and responsibility that a rigid interpretation of fate demands. It doesn't strike us as total nonsense for a radio ad to talk about the possibility of having more control over our fate. When we believe ourselves in the hand of fate, we acknowledge that life is beyond our control; but at the same time, we want to believe that we still have some influence, through conscious decision, over the events that shape our lives.

There are some destructive responses persons make when they become convinced that their lives are dominated by the powers of fate. People take foolish risks in the conviction that, if it is their day to die, they will die whatever they do; and if it is not their day to die, nothing they can do will kill them. Or people accept passively whatever comes. They simply wait for events to unfold in the conviction that nothing a person does will make any difference, so why struggle? Such responses to the notion of fate are destructive. They remove the sense of ambiguity which must be kept if the idea of fate is not to deprive persons of the essential human capacity to make responsible decisions. Fate becomes a demonic notion when it so deprives persons of their humanity.

If fate can have such destructive impact on the perceptions that persons have of themselves and on their ability to deal with the gift of freedom, what accounts for the persistence of the notion of fate? Is it a more or less sophisticated interpretation of existence that enables persons to regress honorably to the dependence of childhood, when they did not have to bear the burden of decisions? The notion of fate serves such a function for some people, but its persistence in human thought cannot be accounted for totally on such grounds. Somehow people have to acknowledge that there are indeed forces at work in the universe and in their lives which are simply beyond their control. The idea of fate persists because, even while persons bear responsibility for their decisions and for what happens to them, they bear that responsibility and make those decisions with a restricted range. There are givens, call them what we will, that are not under our domination.

Thus, life is not fully and completely open to our manipulation. There are limits to what we can do and what we can decide. Not all options we might dream up are really open to us. Nor do we bear responsibility for everything that happens to us. We find ourselves with certain talents and circumstances and backgrounds and opportunities. We are responsible in some measure for what we do with what we have been given, but fate sets the context in which we make those decisions. It is the brutal fact that accidents happen, that limitations are laid on people, that conditions change in ways for which there is no accounting. Recognition of fate is the recognition of the limitations of human existence.

Beyond the limitation of not being able to do this or that particular thing is the ultimate limitation that life itself, and all human energies and efforts and achievements, comes to an end. Everything created by persons passes. Nothing human is eternal. Death is the fate of every living thing, including us. In the word of The Book of Isaiah: "All flesh is grass, and all its beauty is like the flower of the field. The grass withers, the flower fades, when the breath of the Lord blows upon it; surely the people is grass" (40:6-7). A clear perception of this fundamental character of existence drives persons to the acknowledgement of the power beyond their control. One way to speak of that power is to talk of fate.

Jesus raises the question with his disciples: "And which of you by being anxious can add a cubit to his span of life?" It is a corruption of the notion of fate to say that a person's destiny is fixed, no matter what decisions are made or what courses are chosen. There are many things in life, even the extension of its length, over which we do have some measure of control. We can in fact add "cubits" to our span of life. If we drive at reasonable speeds with proper caution and only when we are sober, we may well be adding cubits to the span of life. If we eat in moderation and keep our bodies fit with appropriate exercise, we may well be adding cubits to the span of life. There is risk in all of life, but if we avoid the foolish and the needless and the stupid risks, we may well be adding cubits to the span of life. If we learn how to relax and to let loose of the burdens of our work, we may well be adding cubits to the span of life. If we learn how to deal with the envy, the compulsive need to keep up with others, we may well be adding cubits to the span of life.

But no matter what our efforts or how careful we may be, we do not exercise absolute control over our destiny. The most careful driver may be smashed head-on by a drunken driver. Moderation in eating and regular exercise may not prevent the ravages of cancer. A relaxed style of life may not ward off a fatal heart attack. There are forces that no amount of care or planning can bring under our control, and we live subject to what we may call the forces of fate. Finally we all reach the fated limit of our existence, and no more cubits can be added to the span of life.

The question of Jesus relates to our sense of fate, but is more specific than just a general concern about the limits of life. "And which of you by being anxious can add a cubit to his span of life?" An awareness of the fated character of life may produce anxiety. We may become painfully aware of all the disasters that can happen, events over which we have so little control—the accident that can cripple us, the illness that can incapacitate us, the fire that can wipe out our goods, the theft that can take precious possessions, an economic crisis that can endanger our jobs. All of the possibilities of disaster can stir a deep anxiety within us. When that happens, the question of Jesus helps to bring things back into perspective. "And which of you by being anxious can add a cubit to his span of life?"

If an awareness of the powers of fate can produce anxiety within us, it also happens that we may try to control those powers by means of our anxious worrying. Sometimes we seem to think that if we are only anxious enough, if we only worry enough, we can gain control over the powers that threaten us. We have done all that we can to make a sale, to get ready for an examination, to get a new job, to develop a program. We have prepared the material; we have done our best. Now we should await the outcome calmly, but we cannot. We find ourselves with a sense that, if we are only sufficiently anxious, we can make a difference in what happens. Or the children are out with the car at night, and we sit around with a compulsive sense that if we quit worrying, something bad will happen. There is a subtle but significant difference between loving concern, which knows the dangers of a situation, and compulsive anxiety, which seeks to control a situation inherently beyond control. The question of Jesus helps us to discern the difference. "And which of you by being anxious can add a cubit to his span of life?"

Dealing with fate by reckless abandon or by inert passivity have already been noted as among the less productive ways of responding to the reality that life is not under our control. Allowing anxious fear to dominate our lives is another of those less productive ways. Jesus makes clear that being anxious will not ward off the bad possibilities that the future can hold. Being anxious will not sway the future in our favor. Being anxious will only blight the present. When we are anxious about the future, there seems an unlimited range of possibilities of things that might happen to us. No end appears to the disasters which might befall us, and to begin to worry about all of them moves us into an endless round of anxiety. When we do that, we import into the present a vast range of potential hurts, which in fact will not happen. People have a chance to deal with the things that actually do happen to them. People are overwhelmed when they take on the burden of all the things that might happen to them.

"And which of you by being anxious can add a cubit to your span of life?" The answer to the question is unmistakable. Being anxious will not add one moment to life for anyone. Confronting the question makes us look at how we are dealing with the human condition in which we are subject to powers over which we have no control. The obvious outcome of confronting the question and realizing the answer is for us to cease being anxious. At the beginning of the section in which Jesus asks the question, he admonishes the disciples, "Therefore I tell you, do not be anxious about your life, what you shall eat or what you shall drink, nor about your body, what you shall put on" (Matt. 6:25). Later in the discussion he tells them not to be of anxious mind.

That seems to be the mandate both for the disciples and for us. Do not be anxious about your life. Do not be of anxious mind. But such a mandate may strike us as a useless injunction. To issue such a commandment may seem an exercise in futility. What good does it do to say to us that we should not be anxious? Anxiety is not something we can turn on or off at will. Lord knows, if we could only stop being anxious we would be delighted. But how can we stop being anxious when we ponder the world and our life in it? Injunctions not to be anxious may actually do more harm than good, for we begin to be anxious because we are anxious. Ordering us not to be anxious may only make us even more anxious.

How do we deal with our anxiety? How do we handle the question of Jesus, which forces us to face the uselessness of our worrying? What are we going to do with his injunction not to be anxious? First, it will help if we honestly come to terms with the basic reality of life that we are finite creatures. Certainly we are aware that people are finite, that they are mortal. We know that accidents happen and that everyone will die. But we need to face the fundamental fact, not just intellectually but emotionally and spiritually, until we can live our days in honest recognition. Life on this earth and life for each one of us is fragile; there is no security. Life on this earth and life for each of us is finite; there is no escape from death. Life on this earth and life for each of us is in the context of fate; there are powers at work beyond our control. To accept the given of life instead of struggling against it will help us to ease our anxieties. When we become convinced to the depth of our being that no amount of worry will enable us to escape our fragility or our finitude, it becomes possible to quit worrying about ourselves.

Second, even more important than acceptance of our own finitude is our acceptance of God's care for us. To talk of God's care for us does not deny the fragile, finite, and fated character of our existence. But such talk asserts that beyond our fragility there is the goodness of God, which endures. Beyond our finitude there is the life of God, which is eternal. Such talk asserts that the powers of fate which set the limits of our lives are the powers of the God who loves us. The prophet talked about the withering grass and the fading flowers, but he added another line. "All flesh is grass, and all its beauty is like the flower of the field. The grass withers, the flower fades, when the breath of the Lord blows upon it; surely the people is grass. The grass withers, the flower fades; but the word of our God will stand for ever" (Isaiah 40:6-8).

In the confidence that God's word does stand forever, we can leave the final outcome of our struggles and our endeavors to the divine will. To believe that the powers of fate are not blind or demonic frees us from the profound fear about our ultimate destiny. Jesus tells us that we are not to seek what we are to eat, and he is talking about a consuming, compulsive passion about food. He tells us that we are not to seek what we are to drink. He tells us that we are not to be of anxious mind. Why are we not to be anxious about all these things? "Your Father knows that you need them."

It is a caricature of what Jesus is saying to insist that he is speaking nonsense because obviously people have to work and plan to get the daily necessities of life. Of course they do, and we do. But Jesus is saying that we are not to be anxious about the maintenance and meaning of our lives, for we live out all of our days in the context not of a blind fate but of a loving Father and Mother. There are powers and forces and circumstances in our lives that are beyond our control and that threaten us. To know that life is finally not under our control can produce deep fears. But Jesus Christ offers us an alternative to fear and anxiety. He offers the option of entrusting those things beyond our control to God, whose pleasure it is to give us the Kingdom.

When we find ourselves gripped with worry about all the things that might happen to us, when we are anxious about keeping control over the events of our lives, the question of Jesus can help us to deal with life as it is: "And which of you by being anxious can add a cubit to his span of life?"

3

Why Do You See the Speck?

The Question of Jesus
"Why do you see the speck that is in your brother's eye, but do not notice the log that is in your own eye?" (Luke 6:41).

One of the aberrations of the period of campus unrest during the Vietnam struggle was the scorn which many students heaped on faculty and administrators. Easy cliches about the corruption of anyone over thirty shaped the views many students had of those who were supposed to be their mentors. So widespread and pervasive an attitude is surely an aberration in the long history of relationships between students and faculty. To be sure, some teachers have always commanded more respect and admiration than others, but on every campus in most periods some faculty have been revered and even idolized.

To find people whom we revere and respect is a persistent human need. There need to be role models; there need to be persons who can be emulated; there need to be standard setters who determine appropriate behavior. Many persons play such roles, from college professors to race car drivers, from parents to country music singers, from saints to street toughs. When persons are idolized by others, their virtues are magnified. The college professor is viewed as a truly great person because of her vast learning, her sparkling lectures, her profound books, her wise counsel to students. The baseball player is idolized because of his great athletic skills, and because the kind of life he leads seems to embody all that is dynamic and exciting.

There often comes a moment of shock when people stumble onto the faults of those whom they had held in such high esteem. The college professor who seemed to embody all the human virtues of wisdom and learning and understanding turns out to be terribly indecisive. She simply can't make a decision, and she lets things drift on toward disaster. The baseball player who seemed the embodiment of skill and success turns out to be totally undisciplined in his personal life. He squanders his skills so that far too soon he is unable to meet the demands made on a professional athlete.

Role models and revered figures play a tremendously important part in helping persons give shape to their own lives. Such figures show people some of the options for their own lives and spur them on to the efforts which are required for any genuinely significant achievement. Part of coming to maturity is learning that role models and heroes and idols carry the frailty of being human. They have their faults; they make their mistakes; they blow their opportunities. Even while admiring and emulating those who have served as standards for us, we need a healthy kind of realism about their faults. We need not be naive in accepting the good we see in others. Discernment of the faults of others can keep us from investing too much in them and from loading on them expectations that no finite human being could possibly fulfill. No other persons can be invested with our unlimited and unquestioning confidence. Surely it is a healthy realism to be aware of the essential humanity of every person we deal with, no matter what that person's position or accomplishments. To be human is to be flawed, to have hang-ups, to be limited, to be a mixture of motives.

But if there is a healthy realism about the faults of others, there is also a corrupt compulsion to magnify the faults of others. At some stages of adolescence, there seems to be a need to establish one's own worth by belittling that of others. Teenagers can spend unlimited time in critical analysis of the dress, behavior, and taste of almost everyone they know. Some people never manage to get out of that stage of their development. A man returns from a conference, and from his analysis it can be readily seen that it was a collection of blithering idiots, with one exception of course. Some people seem to live under a compulsion to subject every person they meet to ruthless and destructive criticism, and have become masters of the snide comment about the work such persons do, the house they live in, the way they speak, the behavior of their children. They take obvious delight in listing the faults that others betray. They rejoice in the failures which others suffer. And if by chance they cannot find anything to criticize in public behavior, they raise questions about motives and intentions.

All of us find it easy to criticize others. We harp at the children for the things they do that displease us. We complain about the people with whom we have to work. We are quick to criticize the officials we have elected to run the government. We are adept at discerning the mistakes the neighbors are making in raising their children. Surely the question of Jesus is addressed to us as well as to others. "Why do you see the speck that is in your brother's eye, but do not notice the log that is in your own eye? Or how can you say to your brother, 'Brother, let me take out the speck that is in your eye,' when you yourself do not see the log that is in your own eye?" (Luke 6:41f.).

Why do we see the speck that is in our brother's eye? Why are we so eager in finding the faults of others? Why are we so perceptive in seeing where others fall short? In our more honest moments we can discern a number of reasons why we pay so much attention to the faults of others and take such delight in pointing them out. To point out the faults of others is a way of cutting them down to size. We don't really care for people who come across as too good or too noble or too successful. Too much virtue in another poses a threat to our own self-image. To point out the faults of others is also a way to exalt ourselves. Life for each of us is measured by comparison with others. If others come across as too good, we somehow feel that we are less adequate. If others are exalted, it seems that we are diminished. So we deal with that dynamic in our relationships with others by making sure that the flaws in their character and their behavior are given public notice. We can make ourselves look good simply by picking the right people as the basis of comparison, and we can make ourselves look good by comparing our virtues to their flaws.

Then we use the faults of others as a way of separating ourselves from them, as a way of pushing them off. Having described the flaws of character and conduct in another, we can declare with a measure of self-righteousness that we do not associate with people like that. The faults of others also provide a convenient excuse for not helping them. Judgment that the poor are poor because they are lazy justifies our refusal to offer them aid. When we have pointed out the faults of others, we can well decide that they aren't worth helping. That judgment enables us both to keep our conscience clear and our money pocketed.

Finally, we may use our discernment of the faults of others as a way of exercising control over them. If people accept our judgments about what is wrong with them, it will keep them subservient to us, and it may even be that they will make the effort to become what we want them to be.

When Jesus asks, "Why do you see the speck that is in your brother's eye?" we can certainly answer the question. We've got our reasons for finding fault. But there is another question. "Why do you not notice the log that is in your own eye?" Why are we so blind to the faults in ourselves? Why are we so unwilling to discern our failures? We can answer also this question of Jesus. It is painful to have to acknowledge the corruption in our own lives. We don't like to admit that our motives are mixed, that we have been arrogant and overbearing, that all of our judgments are biased by selfish interest. It is painful to acknowledge the failures we have caused. We don't like to recognize that a relationship is in trouble because of our temper, that the children are alienated because of our insensitivity, that people are turned off because of our arrogance. It just plain hurts to face our own faults, and so we develop an amazing capacity not to see.

Then a clear look at what's wrong with us poses a threat to our identity. We have this image of ourselves as good and virtuous and upright. At least we believe that we are as good as most people. A hard look at what we really are and at what we have done may well shatter that image. Everyone needs a sense of self-worth, and what happens to our sense of our own worth if we look too hard at all the things in our lives for which we can be faulted? How can we maintain any illusion of success if we are too clear-sighted about our failures?

Finally, we are fearful of what others will do to us if we let our weaknesses be known even to ourselves. If we know too well our faults, we may be hindered in moving aggressively to struggle for our own interest and rights. If we acknowledge our faults, others may take advantage of those failures and exploit them to their own gain. Somehow we feel that any authority we may have is tied up with being right, and to admit that we are wrong will cripple us. So when Jesus asks, "Why do you not notice the log that is in your own eye," we can certainly answer the question. We've got our reasons for hiding our faults, even from ourselves.

Do the reasons we offer for seeing the speck in our brother's eye and failing to see the log in our own eye suffice? Having offered our reasons, does that take care of the questions of Jesus and let us move on to other things? After his question, Jesus went on to an admonition. "You hypocrite, first take the log out of your own eye, and then you will see clearly to take out the speck that is in your brother's eye." Our answers really haven't settled the issues raised by the questions of Jesus, and if we take our answers as adequate responses, we haven't let his questions probe our lives very deeply.

We need to let the questions of Jesus become a transforming power in our lives, in the first place, because to focus on the faults of others and to refuse to see our own faults destroys our humanity and corrupts our spirits. There is goodness in all of us, but it becomes a hard, brittle, and even cruel goodness if it is not tempered with the awareness of our frailty. Blindness to the reality of our faults leads to an arrogance of spirit. Self-righteousness is one of the least attractive qualities in the human panorama of unattractive attributes. Such arrogance of spirit sharply limits the possibilities of our relationships with others. If we are always judging others for their faults, we have little capacity to understand them. If we have no awareness of our own frailties, there can be no compassion for others who struggle with their faults. Blind confidence in our own goodness and quick judgments of the faults of others simply make a loving, creative relationship impossible.

In the second place, we need to take seriously the questions of Jesus because only when we become aware of our own failures can there be any healing for us. When we do not know our need for the healing of our spirits, there can be no healing. When we are supremely confident in the righteousness of our lives, it is exceedingly difficult for grace to work within us. The author of Psalm 51 is painfully aware of the sin that has corrupted his life. He is in anguish because he knows the wrongs he has done. He cries out: "For I know my transgressions, and my sin is ever before me." Because he knows his sin with sharp, terrible clarity, he can plead: "Have mercy on me, O God, according to thy steadfast love, according to thy abundant mercy blot out my transgressions. Wash me thoroughly from my iniquity, and cleanse me from my sin." In that cry of desperate need there is hope. Because he wants to be transformed by the power of God, there is an openness to God's grace that can create a clean heart and put a new and right spirit within him.

When we keep our resources as though life were properly founded on possessions, there is little hope of getting free from the demands of things; when we acknowledge our greed, then the grace of God may stir generosity within us. When we find it appropriate for the universe to revolve around us, there is little hope of gaining a more adequate perspective; when we acknowledge our self-centeredness, then the grace of God may move us to compassion. When we are proud of our virtue, there is little hope of being saved from our self-righteousness; when we acknowledge our arrogance, then the grace of God may grant us humility. When we are confident in our strength, there is little hope that we can escape the need to dominate every situation that threatens us; when we acknowledge our weakness, then the grace of God may grant us strength.

In the third place, we need to take seriously the questions of Jesus because only when we know our weaknesses can we be of help to others. We can't help others so long as we are pretending to a super-human goodness. We can minister to others when we share their humanity with its goodness and its evil, its strengths and its weaknesses. When we have opened our lives in penitence to the healing grace of God, then we have something to offer. After the psalmist acknowledges his transgressions, and after he prays for a clean heart and a right spirit, he can offer: "Then I will teach transgressors thy ways, and sinners will return to thee." After our own lives are made right, we have the hope of being able to offer something to others. "First take the log out of your own eye, and then you will see clearly to take out the speck that is in your brother's eye." Jesus directs us toward ministry to one another, and to helping one another deal with the corruptions that have distorted life. But we are able to help only when we know and have dealt with the sin within our own life.

As we look at who we are and how we deal with others, there is an urgency about the question of Jesus. "Why do you see the speck that is in your brother's eye, but do not notice the log that is in your own eye? Or how can you say to your brother, 'Brother, let me take out the speck that is in your eye,' when you yourself do not see the log that is in your own eye?"

4

Why Are You Afraid?

The Question of Jesus
"Why are you afraid? Have you no faith?" (Mark 4:40).

Reporters frequently find it difficult to ask pertinent or appropriate questions. A couple whose young son's body has just been pulled from the river probably ought not to be interviewed on television at all. Such an interview demands more sensitivity than most reporters seem to possess, for they are liable to ask the parents such questions as, "How do you feel?" In other circumstances reporters do not always break through with the most penetrating inquiries. There is the reporter who asked the couple who had just won a million dollars in the lottery, "Are you happy?" There is the reporter who asked the candidate for mayor, "Are you in favor of reducing crime in the city?"

A question Jesus asked his disciples on one occasion would seem to fall into the category of foolish questions. One night he and the disciples were going across the Sea of Galilee, " and a great storm of wind arose, and the waves beat into the boat, so that the boat was already filling" (Mark 4:37). Jesus was asleep through the whole business. When they finally awoke him, he stilled the wind and the waves, and then he asked them, "Why are you afraid?" It does sound like a silly question. Just why did he think they wouldn't be afraid, out in the middle of the sea at night in a boat filling up with water? It's a little bit like asking someone who is holding an airplane up by pulling on the arm rests why he is afraid. There's fear that the plane is going to fall out of the sky, of course. There is fear because it is obvious to any right-thinking person that nothing as big as a 747 can get off the ground. There is fear because the person is convinced that he is pushing his luck every time he gets in an airplane and is certain that one day his luck will run out. For anyone with an unshakable conviction that only by the sheer effort of his will the plane stays up at all, it is a little foolish to ask, "Why are you afraid?"

Confronted with the question "Why are you afraid?" many people have no problem in coming up with an answer. To ask the question as though there should be anything surprising about their fears would indicate to them that the questioner is really out of touch with what life is. After all, life is a fearful affair. There are many threats which can send chills of panic through any person who has the least awareness of what is going on.

There is the fear of accidents. We don't have to get on an airplane to place our lives in jeopardy. Every time we get in a car there is the real possibility of a serious accident. We don't even have to leave home to risk an accident. "Why are you afraid?" Just think about all the accidents that happen every day.

There is the fear of illness. To contemplate all the things that can go wrong with the human body is to open up a vast abyss of pain and suffering. Who knows when illness may strike? Who knows when that little pain signifies that something serious is happening? "Why are you afraid?" Just look at all the people who are ill, and think of all the things that can happen to a person. If it's not diabetes, it's cancer. If it's not cancer, it's a heart attack.

There is the fear of death. Death is a certainty, but we do everything possible to postpone it and to hide it. Death is universal, but that does not make it less frightening. We are afraid of death because death cuts us off from the life we have known. Death is frightening because it is so lonely. There is strength and comfort in sharing experiences with others, but every person experiences death alone. We fear death because it is the unknown. However painful or unpleasant this life may be, we at least know what we are facing. But death confronts us with a totally new dimension. In spite of the accounts that persons have given of their state when they were very close to death, no one has ever passed through the final barrier and returned to tell us what it is like. "Why are you afraid?" In the rare moments of gripping awareness that death comes not just to everyone but to me, we are fearful.

There is the fear of failure. When we venture into any new or significant undertaking, there is always the possibility of failure.

The only way to avoid the risk of failure is to refuse to venture into anything which challenges our abilities. But if we do venture into enterprises that make meaningful demands on us, we always know that we may fail. We may fail as we take the risk of starting a new business. We may fail as we take on the responsibility of being parents. We may fail if we get up to make a speech. And the possibility of failure is frightening. It threatens our confidence; it threatens our self-identity; it threatens the confidence other people have in us; it threatens the potential we have for the future. "Why are you afraid?" There is the possibility of failure in this enterprise, and the consequences of failure are serious indeed.

There is the fear involved in our relationships with others. When we enter into significant relationships with others, there must be a large measure of trust. We depend on others to be loyal to us and to protect our interests, and others depend on us to be loyal to them and to protect their interests. When we entrust ourselves to others we become vulnerable, for if they fail us, the hurt can be painful. No matter how trustworthy people have shown themselves to be in the past, in the frailty of human relationships there is always the possibility that a trust will be violated. As we contemplate all that could happen, there can be profound fear of what others might do to us because we have become so dependent on them. But there is also the fear that we might violate the trust others have placed in us. All too well, we know the possibility that we will fail in our commitments when the pressures get too great, and we are frightened about the possible harm that we can do to others. "Why are you afraid?" Because we are so dependent on others, and others are so dependent on us, and we may fail one another.

There is fear for others. Parents know the chill of fear on the night a child is an hour late coming home from a car trip with a group of young people. It is not only our own illness or failure or death that makes us fearful, but the prospect of illness or failure or death of those we love deeply. We fear for a spouse; we fear for a parent; we fear for a child; we fear for a friend. Life is enriched by the bonds of love which unite us with others, but when we love we become vulnerable because what hurts another hurts us. "Why are you afraid?" Just think of all the things that might happen to those we care about deeply.

Life indeed is fearful, and there are plenty of good reasons to be afraid. If anyone really wants to know why we are afraid, we have no problem in citing good reasons. If anyone asks why we

30

are afraid as though it were foolish to allow fears to be part of our lives, we can only respond that it must be obvious to anyone who sees the precariousness of life why people are afraid. On most occasions when we know fear, it is as obvious why we fear as it is obvious why the disciples were afraid out in the boat that night. There was a clear and present danger. So the question of Jesus does sound a bit foolish when he asks them in the middle of a storm with the boat filling with water: "Why are you afraid?"

It is always a bit risky, however, to assume that Jesus was running around asking silly questions. Before simply dismissing the whole business, we will do well to ask what Jesus might have intended by asking his disciples out in the middle of the sea in a leaky boat why they were afraid.

Jesus was obviously concerned that the disciples were afraid in that situation, for because of their fear, they had not coped with the situation well. It is no small matter for people to have their days dominated by fear. Fear does tragic things to persons. Fear keeps us from running the risks that are inherent in all creative and challenging living. Or if we do venture in spite of the fear, the fear can keep us from the abandon and freedom that will make success possible. Fear often brings to pass the very thing that is feared. Because of our fear, we may refuse to enter into relationships with others that would be fulfilling both for us and for them. Fear of the future becomes a blight on the present. To allow fear to grip our lives subjects us to a terrible master that controls and dominates us. So when Jesus asked his disciples, and when he asks us, "Why are you afraid?" it is not a casual or idle question. The impact of fear on the lives of people is far too serious to deal with it in casual or idle fashion.

"Why are you afraid?" With that question, Jesus immediately asked another: "Why are you afraid? Have you no faith?" By putting those two questions together, Jesus focuses for the disciples and for us the relation between fear and faith. In essence, Jesus was asking the disciples if they believed that he could care for them. When the storm broke, Jesus was asleep in the boat, and apparently the tumult didn't awaken him. But at length the disciples awoke him and cried out to him, "Teacher, do you not care if we perish?" There was the root of their fear. There was the reason why Jesus asked them why they were afraid. They didn't know whether Jesus cared whether they perished or not, and because they didn't know that, they were afraid. "And he awoke and rebuked the wind and said to the sea, 'Peace! Be still!' And the wind ceased, and there was a great calm." When the disciples saw what Jesus had done, they were astonished at this display of power. "And they were filled with awe, and said to one another, 'Who then is this, that even wind and sea obey him?'" (Mark 4:38-41).

The disciples saw in Jesus' action in stilling the wind and the sea the evidence of his power over even the forces of nature. God has made him Lord of all, and even the powers of this world are obedient to him. The New Testament witness to the life of Jesus does not portray him spending his time impressing people with his powers to control the natural world. He didn't run around making rain when crops needed it or providing nice days for picnics. His power over the forces of nature does serve for us as a symbol of the power he can have over the internal storms which sweep through our lives from time to time. When we are buffeted by events that crowd in on our lives, Jesus can bring a calm and peace to our spirits. When we are engulfed by a deep despair, Jesus can still the tumult within us. When we are lost in a terrible darkness, Jesus can bring his light into our lives.

Because Jesus has such power in our lives, he can help us deal with our fears, even as the stilling of the storm on the Sea of Galilee allayed the fears of his disciples. Many of our fears result from threats to what are essentially selfish desires. We are afraid of losing the things we have grasped in our greed. The presence of Jesus Christ in our lives helps us to deal with our selfishness. In his presence we gain a perspective on the things we have and see them in their true worth, not with the inflated value we often give to them. Many of our fears have to do with our uncertainty about who we are. Failure threatens us so severely because we tend to identify our worth with our successes. The fear of rejection poses such threats to us because we are dependent on the approval of others for our confidence. Jesus Christ helps us to know our worth, not because we have succeeded or because others approve of us, but because we are known and cared for by God. Many of our fears have to do with our failures in love. Because we close ourselves in with mistrust and hatred, we are indeed threatened by those who challenge us. In his love for us, Jesus enables us to become more loving and thus less fearful. As the author of First John wrote: "There is no fear in love, but perfect love casts out fear. For fear has to do with punishment, and he who fears is not perfected in love. We love because he first loved us" (1 John 4:18-19).

Jesus Christ helps us to love, and thus to be free from the fears that blight our lives. To love God is to have confidence in God's care for us and to ease our fears about life and death. To love others is to be surrounded by a community of caring and trusting people who bring a sense of confidence into life and eases our fears. To love ourselves is to be free from the threats to our own sense of identity.

"Why are you afraid?" Even when we can give what appear to be perfectly good reasons for our fear, Jesus presses the question at us. Why do we let things frighten us and bring such fear into our lives? "Why are you afraid? Have you no faith?" Why don't we trust in the power and the goodness of God? The care of Jesus for us, the love of God in our lives will not spare us from all the things that bring suffering and pain and even death. But within the context of faith, we don't have to be so fearful of all those things. In Jesus Christ we come to know that even suffering can be used by God for creative and redemptive work. In Jesus Christ we come to know that pain can be endured with nobility and courage through the sustaining presence of God. In Jesus Christ we come to know that even death is not to be feared as shattering all our hopes, but that God brings the victory of divine purpose through death.

Fear of all that the future might bring to us puts a blight over the whole of life. When we are fearful about the future, there are an unlimited number of things that can make us afraid. Thomas Kepler once wrote: "Some of us would do well to emulate the woman who realized that her fears were ruining her life, so she made for herself a 'worry table.' In tabulating her worries she discovered that 40% will never happen; 30% were about all decisions which cannot be altered; 12% were about others' criticisms of me, most untrue; 10% were about my health, which gets worse as I worry; 8% were legitimate since life has some real problems to meet."[1] Such an observation is helpful in getting our fears into some realistic perspective, for we are fearful of many things that never come to be. But as we are able to nurture within us our confidence in God and God's care, we are increasingly able to face the present and the future without fear whatever may come.

Whatever the circumstances of our life, the question of Jesus is not foolish. "Why are you afraid?" Why are you afraid of all the accidents that might happen? Most of them won't, and those that do can be dealt with in the courage granted by the grace of God. Why are you afraid of all the illnesses that might strike? Most of them will not come to you, and those that do can be met in the strength granted by the grace of God. Why are you afraid of failures? Most of them won't happen, and those that do will not change your place in the love of God. Why are you afraid of death? It will come, but through the resurrection of Jesus Christ there is the promise of the new life through death.

"Why are you afraid? Have you no faith?"

5

Why Do You Not Understand?

The Question of Jesus
"Why do you not understand what I say?" (John 8:43).

After a rather lengthy discussion on one occasion, Jesus asked with obvious vehemence, "Why do you not understand what I say?" Why don't you grasp what is going on? Why isn't it clear to you what is being said? When such a question is asked of us, there are times when we correctly respond that we don't understand because the person speaking hasn't communicated.

Hyde Park in London serves as a forum for all kinds of speakers dealing with all kinds of issues, including religion. Donald Soper, one of the outstanding preachers in England, used to go regularly to the park to preach. Unlike most congregations, people who listen in Hyde Park are ready to engage the preacher in lively and vigorous exchange. Mr. Soper has written of some of his experiences in dealing with the people who listened as he preached. On one occasion a heckler took issue with what he was saying and asked Soper to prove that he wasn't crazy for being a Christian. Not quite sure how to deal with that and in order to gain a little time, Soper responded by asking the man to prove that he wasn't crazy. The man promptly pulled out a discharge from a mental hospital. Then there was a faithful heckler who used to sit on the wall beside him every time he preached. Soper reports that when he would get some tough question to deal with, his words tended to get longer, his sentences tended to get more involved, his thought tended to get more abstract. When he would finish dealing with a question in such a fashion, the heckler would inevitably ask the crowd: "Now is that perfectly clear?"

Sometimes we don't understand because those who seek to interpret the faith to us simply fail to make it clear. Theologians and preachers develop their own specialized language and concepts. As with any field or endeavor, theology must use technical language, and theologians can get on with their enterprise only if they can use terms with highly specialized meanings. But if theologians and preachers are going to deal with those who are not professionals in the field, they must learn to put what they are talking about in a form that others can understand.

The problem of communication is a matter not only of language but also of convoluted thought. "We direct the glance of apprehension and theoretical inquiry to pure consciousness in its own absolute Being. It is this which remains over as the 'phenomenological residuum' we were in quest of: remains over, we say, although we have 'suspended' the whole world with all things, living creatures, men, ourselves included. We have literally lost nothing, but have won the whole of Absolute Being, which, properly understood, conceals in itself as transcendencies, 'constituting' them within itself." As the man said, "Now is that perfectly clear?" "Why do you not understand?" Because you haven't succeeded in stating your ideas in a comprehensible way.

Sometimes we fail to understand the claims and affirmation of the Christian faith because the world view and the culture of the biblical period are so different from our own. The Christian faith is rooted in the tradition of Israel, and the events that shaped the faith took place at a particular time in history and at a particular place in our world. That time and place are different from the time and place we know, so that much that we encounter in the Bible seems strange to us. Here is a world in which demons possess people and cause all manner of strange behavior and illness. Here is a universe in which hell is a real place down in the bowels of the earth, and heaven is a real place just above the firmament that overarches the earth. Here is a world in which things happen because God decrees that they shall happen.

God's relation with the world then strikes us as quite different from the way in which we understand God to deal with us now. God calls directly to people and tells them in unmistakable terms to do this or to do that. God intervenes directly in the processes of nature: The sun stands still, the waters of the Red Sea part, the wind and the waves quiet down at a word from Jesus. God intervenes directly in the processes of history. It is God who sends the Assyrians to punish the people: "Ah, Assyria, the rod of my anger, the staff of my fury! Against a godless nation I send him, and against the people of my wrath I command him, to take spoil and seize plunder, and to tread them down like the mire of the streets" (Isa. 10:5-6).

Such a world is really not our world. When astronauts roam into space, we know that they don't find heaven "up there." We may talk about demon-possessed people, but we don't go around trying to get little creatures to leave people who are sick. When we try to understand the things that happen in the world around us, we look for causes within the orderly processes we have discerned. When we try to interpret the events of history, we look for economic pressures, political factors, powerful personalities. We are not given to writing history by indicating that God causes this to happen or that to take place. "Why do you not understand?" Because it's such a strange and different world you lead me into when we enter the world of the Bible.

Sometimes we fail to understand because we are dealing with concerns that stretch the limits of our minds and our imaginations. The world of the "known" has been constantly expanding as people probe with evermore sophisticated instruments and concepts into the universe in which we find ourselves. Much that confronted earlier generations as a mystery has become knowable and controllable. But always beyond the known there is the mystery of the unknown. However far we probe into the wonders of the world around us, there are realities beyond the range of our understanding, which we cannot explain or control. The capacity of persons to learn and the accelerated ability to deal with this world are cuase for rejoicing, yet we must never entertain the illusion that we have mastered all of creation.

Beyond what we know, there are mysteries we can glimpse that puzzle us. Beyond the mysteries we can glimpse, there may well be infinite complexities which are totally beyond our awareness. We dare not limit reality to that which is open to our capacities. Clifton Fadiman put it this way: "The most apparent thing about us is that we live amid the unapparent. How tiny are the five ports of our senses set against the vast mysterious coastline of the invisible. The past and the future—the two countries in which we mainly live—are invisible. Our minds, which make us persons, are unseen by us. We live on a gigantic sphere of which only a pinpoint is sensible to us at any moment. Our very bodies, which seem so palpable, are for the most part invisible. All children should be given a sense of the invisible. At an early age take your child into a dark room, insert a flashlight into your mouth, show him the bony caverns of the skull wierdly lit in a reddish glow. It will do more for him than television."[2]

A sense of the mystery beyond our reach and an awareness that there may be vast ranges beyond what our senses can grasp, relate us to the essential character of the religious dimension of life. When we are concerned with the fundamental faith by which we live, we are inevitably dealing with the wondrous and the mysterious. It is through faith that we finite creatures relate to the infinite, we mortal creatures relate to the eternal. But we do not escape our finitude or our mortality. We have glimpsed something of the eternal dimension of life, but we don't grasp it. We have known the longing for meaning, but we don't define it. We have sensed the reality and the presence of God, but we don't control the divine. Finally, we live by faith and not by knowledge. Ultimately we live on the basis of promises and not by certainties. "Why do you not understand?" Because we are dealing with a range of reality and meaning beyond our understanding.

Sometimes we fail to understand because we haven't tried to understand, because we haven't made the effort required to understand. In any significant realm of human learning, discipline and effort are demanded in order to grasp the intricacies of the field. Years of study are required to know how the human body functions. Endless hours of practice are demanded before the notes on a page can be translated into music. Disciplined effort is necessary for one to become sensitive to the expressions of the human spirit. The significant meanings of life are not readily apparent to casual observation. The ways of God are not to be grasped by the dilettante. Jesus said to the people: "You seek to kill me, because my word finds no place in you" (John 8:37). It wasn't just that they didn't hear him. It wasn't just that they rejected what they heard. They didn't let his word find a place in them. They didn't let it dwell within them until they grasped what he was talking about and who he was.

If we do not understand the truth of God and the ways of God, it may be because we have not invested enough of ourselves in the effort to understand. We begin to grasp the ways of God only when we are willing to listen. It is not easy to listen. It is very difficult to hear what another person is saying to us, and we have to pay careful attention to discern the mind and spirit of the person through the words that are spoken. God speaks to us, but to be able to discern what is said demands our sensitive attention. Paying attention requires thought about what we have heard and reflection to try to probe the meaning. To hear the word of God we need to take that word into our lives until it becomes a part of us.

Full understanding in any area of human knowledge requires the skill and experience of the expert. Comprehension of nuclear physics and psychiatry and the history of art is possible only for those who have the gifts and who have devoted the time required. Unlike this kind of knowledge, the knowledge of God is not limited to the experts. There are people who devote their lives to exploring the scripture or developing theological statements. But the knowledge of God does not require special expertise or learning. It does require persons who are open to the expressions of God in our world, persons who are willing to let the word of God dwell within them, persons who will invest themselves in the effort to discern who God is and what God is doing.

In George Bernard Shaw's *Saint Joan* King Charles complained to Joan: "Why don't the voices come to me? I am the king, not you." Joan replied: "They do come to you; but you do not hear them. You have not sat in the field in the evening listening for them. When the angelus rings you cross yourself and have done with it; but if you prayed from your heart, and listened to the thrilling of the bells in the air after they stop ringing, you would hear the voices as well as I do."[3] "Why do you not understand?" Because we have not paid attention, and listened, and been sensitive, and made the effort required to understand.

Sometimes we fail to understand because we don't want to understand. Jesus told the people with whom he was in conversation: "If God were your Father, you would love me, for I proceeded and came forth from God; I came not of my own accord, but he sent me" (John 8:42). Surely it is possible to discern God in many ways—in the wonder of the world around us, in the lingering beauty of the sound of the bells, in the silent moment of meditation, in the word of the prophet. But for the Christian, the full expression of God is through Jesus Christ. Jesus is the expression of the wonder, the truth, the goodness, and the mystery of God. He came from God, and God sent him into our world to bring the richness of God's love. After Jesus had declared to the people how he had come from God, he asked them the question: "Why do you not understand what I say?" Here was Jesus speaking the word of God, speaking to them of what he had seen of God. Here was Jesus offering to set people free from their slavery to sin. Here was Jesus expressing in his words and life the truth of God. But they would not understand who he was or what he was doing.

Jesus asked the question about why they did not understand, and Jesus also answered the question. "Why do you not understand what I say? It is because you cannot bear to hear my word. You are of your father the devil, and your will is to do your father's desires. . . . He who is of God hears the words of God; the reason why you do not hear them is that you are not of God" (John 8:43, 44, 47). We fail to understand—not simply because things aren't made clear to us, nor because the world of the Bible is such a strange world, nor because we are dealing with profound mysteries beyond our comprehension, nor because we haven't made the effort to understand. We don't understand because we don't want to understand, because we cannot bear to understand. Mark Twain once commented that it wasn't the part of the Bible he didn't understand that bothered him but the part of the Bible that he did understand.

We sense rightly that if we did understand what Jesus Christ is saying to us it would have profound impact on our lives. We have heard enough to know that if we really understood what God is making known to us through Jesus, great claims would be made on our lives. We don't want to understand the ways of God because then God's ways would become our ways, and we grasp tightly the ways we already have. If we let the truth of God in Christ permeate our lives, then giving instead of getting will become the style by which we operate, then loyalty to God and to others will be asked of us, then the goodness of God will become the orientation of our lives, then love will be the power we seek to express in all that we do and say. Because the claims of God threaten our self-centered lives, we don't really want to understand.

"Why do you not understand?" Well, we have our reasons. But Jesus Christ is there in the midst of our lives and of our community, witnessing to the truth and goodness and love of God. By God's grace, it may yet be that we will understand who we are and what God has given to us.

6

Why Put Me to the Test?

The Question of Jesus
"But Jesus, aware of their malice, said, 'Why put me to the test, you hypocrites?'" (Matt. 22:18).

We may talk about the folly of naive trust. Gullible people are constantly being swindled by those who prey upon the trusting. A repeated story in the newspaper tells of the person who took his or her life savings out of the bank and gave them to a complete stranger. A confidence game frequently involves several dynamics as the crook works to take advantage of the victim. There is often an appeal to greed as the victim is offered the opportunity to get a lot of easy money. All the person has to do is put up some money to show good faith. There is frequently an appeal to the willingness to help others.

Clergy are prime targets for those who try to get money by seeking support for worthy but fictitious causes, for presumably clergy are strongly motivated to try to help others. Such an altrustic impulse is easily exploited. There is almost always a sense of urgency in the scheme. The opportunity to get a lot of money or the chance to meet a human need must be grasped immediately. The operator of a confidence game wants to give the victim as little time as possible to think about what is being offered, or to ask whether the whole enterprise is sensible. Finally, there is the necessity to establish an atmosphere of trust. Often this is done by having an accomplice who comes on the scene at the appropriate moment with an enthusiastic response to the scheme proposed. The accomplice will agree to put up money so that the victim will be encouraged to trust enough to put up money also.

In many circumstances, to be too trusting is naive and foolish. A person does well to check the credentials of a door-to-door salesperson, for there are those who peddle shoddy products or who take down-payments and deliver no product at all. A person does well to get guarantees in writing and to read warranties with care, for promises boldly made at the time of the sale may not be honored when something goes wrong. A person does well to test the claims people make about themselves. There was a student expelled from school, not because he couldn't do the work but because he failed to apply himself. After a year the student applied for readmission, claiming that he was now highly motivated. But he could offer no evidence from what he had done during the year away to substantiate the claim that he had changed significantly. The committee considering his application refused the admission until he had done something to support the claim that he was now ready to do serious academic work.

To be too trusting is naive and foolish, for there are people who will take advantage of others. There are people who deliberately set out to deceive others for their own gain. There are people who do not reveal their true intentions. There are people who hide who they are and what they are about. It is appropriate and necessary to test people to find out who they are and what they will do, to find out what their credibility has been in the past, to find out how they have dealt with the people who have trusted them in other situations.

If we may talk about the folly of naive trust, we may also talk about the folly of cynical distrust. If we can be foolish in our trust of others, we can also be foolish in our refusal to trust others. There are relationships crucial to our humanity that can be established only on the basis of trust in other people. There are people who choose to live in comparative isolation, to be sure. But life for most of us is nurtured and enriched through the relationships we have with others. In marriage we make an unending and unconditional commitment to one other person. Parents and children continue their care for each other even when sheer physical survival is not at stake. Persons bind their lives together through ties of friendship. People find it both expedient and meaningful to carry on their work in close contact with others. Students and teachers find that learning is enhanced when they share a common quest for truth and understanding. In countless ways and in varied situations, our lives are intertwined with those who share some dimension of common experience with us.

There is something deeply wrong if we have to be constantly testing the other in relationships such as these. It is not a sign of health in a marriage if one partner is always asking the other to prove his or her love, if one partner is continually checking to be certain that the other is faithful. There comes the time when a parent must trust a child in the expectation that the child is capable of making the decisions that have to be made. If friends are always probing and testing each other to see whether they are really loyal, there is little meaning left in the friendship. Persons in business together who must spend energy checking on the integrity of one another cripple the common enterprise. If teachers and students believe that they are being misled by one another, the quest for truth and knowledge suffers severely. People can bind their lives together in meaningful and significant ways only when they are able to trust each other.

To be sure, because we are human and because we must deal with other human beings, any trust can be violated. People who are close to each other do fail in their loyalty and love. Marriage vows are broken, and the promises which have been the basis of their life together are not honored. The trust that parents and children put in one another turns out to be misplaced. Friendship implies responsibilites to each other, and those responsibilities are not met. Persons use a business relationship to exploit and to take advantage of one another. Teachers and students reveal their blindness and allow selfish interests to corrupt their quest for truth.

But in spite of the failures of persons in all kinds of relationships, we destroy the possibility of significant contact with another if we become cynical and distrust every word another speaks and every deed another does. If we are going to realize the potential for good in being with others, we have to run the risk of trusting them. Properly there is a time of testing when we meet others. There is prudent care in making ourselves vulnerable to others. But beyond the time of testing, we must live with trust. Tragedy is when a person has been so badly wounded by the perfidy of others that trust is no longer a possibility.

Certainly we can be too naive in accepting the word and the promise of others. But if it is a mark of sophistication to be cynical, we can blight our lives by developing a sophistication which discerns ulterior motives and destructive intent in every word and deed of others.

If there is properly a time of testing as we enter into relationships with other persons, does it make sense to use our human experience in interpreting what happens between God and ourselves? Is there a time of testing in our relationship with God? In the account of the travels of the Israelites after Moses led them out of their captivity in Egypt, there came a time when they wanted to put God to the test. They had moved into the wilderness and were camped at a place called Rephidim. When they stopped there, they found to their dismay that there was no water. "Therefore the people found fault with Moses, and said, 'Give us water to drink.' And Moses said to them, 'Why do you find fault with me? Why do you put the Lord to the proof?'" Moses heard the people demanding that God prove that they were cared for. He had brought them out here in the wilderness. Surely the people had a point when they faced a crisis so that they murmured against Moses: "Why did you bring us up out of Egypt, to kill us and our children and our cattle with thirst?" (Exod. 17:2-3). If God had really gotten them into this enterprise, let God get some water to keep them from dying. Put God to the test. Let God show that the claims and promises will be fulfilled.

There came the time when the Pharisees tested Jesus to see if they could get him to say something that would be damaging to him. "Then the Pharisees went and took counsel how to entangle him in his talk. And they sent their disciples to him, along with the Herodians, saying, 'Teacher, we know that you are true, and teach the way of God truthfully, and care for no man; for you do not regard the position of men. Tell us, then, what you think. Is it lawful to pay taxes to Caesar, or not?'" (Matt. 22:15-17). They were putting Jesus to the test to see how he would handle a controversial issue and to see if they could get him in trouble. If Jesus said that they shouldn't pay taxes, he would certainly be in trouble with the authorities. If he said that they should pay taxes, he might well lose the support of some of the more radical groups among his people.

Surely there are times for all of us when we want to test God, when we have an urgent need to find out whether there really is anything to all this talk about God and what God can do. If we are not so bold as to put God directly to the test, we may find ourselves testing those who claim to speak on God's behalf. Can what is claimed about God and what God does be checked out in the "real" world. Does it square with the experience we have had? Can the promises of God be counted on? Is the power of God capable of doing what is claimed for it? Our testing of God may take many forms. The Israelites demanded that God provide water for them when they were stuck in a barren place in the wilderness. The Pharisees plotted to see how Jesus would handle the question they put to him. In the time of our anguish, we may test God by demanding that God give proof by healing us of our illness or by taking from us our pain. In the time of our anxiety, we may test God by pressing that God enable us to succeed in accomplishing the hard task before us. In the time of our uncertainty, we may test God by insisting that God show us what to do in the decision we have to make. To want proof from God is a pervasive human longing. If only God would make clear the divine character and purpose and power. We are tempted to say, "We will believe, Lord, if you will only meet the test we are setting before you."

There is probably such a time of testing for most of us in our relationship with God. But the scripture points us toward that relationship with God in which we go beyond the test to trust. After the people of Israel complained about the water, Moses went to God and complained bitterly: "What shall I do with this people? They are almost ready to stone me?" God told Moses to strike the rock at Horeb, and that water would come from it for the people to drink. Moses did as God told him, and the water did come. But then Moses chastized the people as he named the place where the people had tested God and God had met their demands. "And he called the name of the place Massah [which means "proof"] and Meribah [which means "contention"], because of the faultfinding of the children of Israel, and because they put the Lord to the proof by saying, 'Is the Lord among us or not?'" (Exod. 17:4, 7). God met their demand for proof by providing water, but the demand itself was clear evidence of the lack of trust and understanding. By their testing of God they were distorting their relationship with God. They should have known God and God's care for them well enough that they didn't have to test it or demand proof of it. God doesn't constantly have to be providing proof by meeting their demands for evidence.

Jesus interpreted rightly the question of the Pharisees about the payment of the taxes. The scripture is clear about their motives. "The Pharisees went and took counsel how to entangle him in his talk." They were trying to discredit Jesus by testing him. They were not asking the question in an effort to gain understanding and insight. Jesus was aware of what was going on. "But Jesus, aware of their malice, said, 'Why put me to the test, you hypocrites.'" They were trying to trip him up. They were testing him as a way of resisting him. They were testing him with a foregone conclusion already clear in their minds. Because they adopted such a stance toward Jesus, they were unable to grasp who he was and what he was doing. They never got beyond testing him for their own malicious purposes.

Where are we in our relationship with God? Are we still having to test him, or have we grown to the point of trust? From all the evidence of God's care, from all of the witness of the goodness of God, are we ready to trust that God loves us and wills the best for us? Have we moved beyond the need of demanding evidence on our terms of the reality and power of God so that we can accept with quiet confidence that we are indeed cared for?

How do we answer the question of Jesus? "Why put me to the test?" Do we too test Jesus as a way of resisting him? The claims of God in Christ on our lives may come as a threat. We don't really want to let Jesus Christ become our Lord, and so we devise tests that we demand to be met before we will believe. There is an astonishing arrogance about such behavior, as though Jesus really had to prove himself to us. We put Jesus to the test because it is a way of keeping him at a distance from us.

Do we test Jesus because we have real question about his goodness and his love. From all that is known of Jesus and how he dealt with people, can there really be question about his honest concern for others? Here was a man who dealt compassionately, mercifully, honestly with all the people he encountered. Here was a man who loved his people enough to die for them on a cross. Do we really have to test whether Jesus spoke and acted with passionate and loving concern?

Do we test Jesus because we have question that he expresses the character and power of God? Is there a suspicion in our minds that he is a fraud who didn't really embody the grace and truth of God? From the time that he walked on this earth through all the ages of Christian history, people have perceived in him that here was the breaking in of the infinite into this finite world, here was the eternal embodied in the life of a human being. Jesus spoke of God his Father, and interpreted his own life and ministry as coming from God. Do we really have to test whether Jesus is in fact the expression of God in our world?

Do we test Jesus because we have real question about the truth he manifested? His life expresses the fulfillment of human existence. In him we see the manifestation of what life on this earth can be. He lived out fully the meaning for which we grope as we try to understand our own lives. Do we really have to test whether Jesus fulfilled the purpose of God for human life?

The Pharisees sent disciples to test Jesus with the question about whether to pay taxes to Caesar. Later the Pharisees came to Jesus themselves, "And one of them, a lawyer, asked him a question to test him. 'Teacher, which is the great commandment in the law?' And he said to him, 'You shall love the Lord your God with all your heart, and with all your soul, and with all your mind. This is the great and first commandment'" (Matt. 22:37-38). When we have come to love the Lord our God with heart and soul and mind, we don't have to test him any more; we live in the quiet trust and confidence of God's love for us.

7

Could You Not Watch One Hour?

The Question of Jesus
"And he came to the disciples and found them sleeping; and he said to Peter, 'So, could you not watch with me one hour?'" (Matt. 26:40).

One of life's more trying experiences occurs when we have to stay awake and find the demands for sleep almost irresistible. The head nods until it suddenly jerks up again. The eyelids droop until they are forced up by sheer willpower. The body shifts around in the effort to find a position that will encourage wakefulness. Effort is made to concentrate attention on what is going on, but it turns out to be a difficult matter indeed to stay alert. It is hard enough to fight the battle against sleep when we are alone; it becomes even more difficult when we are in a social situation that limits the measures we can take.

There was an occasion when faculty members of a school were put through what could only be called cruel and unusual suffering. Following a large dinner and a rather lengthy program around the tables, the guests of the school adjourned to the auditorium for a lecture by a distinguished German theologian. An academic procession preceded the lecture and ended with the members of the faculty in full academic regalia sitting behind the lecturer on the platform. The hour was late; the room was hot; the lecture was involved and difficult to follow; the lecturer's English was heavily accented. All of that conspired to make staying awake extraordinarily difficult. Some of us in the audience managed to keep ourselves awake only by watching with some amusement and sympathy the struggles of those on the platform. Major attention focused on one rather elderly faculty member, for there was clearly the strong possibility that he would fall completely out of his chair.

We can sympathize with the plight of Peter and James and John. After Jesus had eaten the last meal he was to have with the disciples, he took them to a place called Gethsemane. There he left most of the disciples, but he took with him Peter and James and John as he went on farther to pray. "Then he said to them, 'My soul is very sorrowful, even to death; remain here, and watch with me.' And going a little farther he fell on his face and prayed, 'My Father, if it be possible, let this cup pass from me; nevertheless, not as I will, but as thou wilt.' And he came to the disciples and found them sleeping; and he said to Peter, 'So, could you not watch with me one hour? Watch and pray that you may not enter into temptation; the spirit indeed is willing, but the flesh is weak'" (Matt. 26:38-41). Twice more Jesus went away alone to pray, and each time when he came back he found the disciples asleep, even though he had asked them to watch with him.

There is a poignancy about the question of Jesus to Peter and the others. "So, could you not watch with me one hour?" It seemed important to Jesus that these three closest to him stay awake and pray with him. There was obvious disappointment when Jesus came and found that they had fallen asleep. Was it asking too much that in this night of his crisis they stay awake and watch with him? Jesus needed them, and they needed to be preparing themselves for what was coming to them. "Watch and pray that you may not enter into temptation; the spirit indeed is willing, but the flesh is weak." But each time when Jesus returned from his own time of prayer, he found them asleep, "for their eyes were heavy."

"Could you not watch one hour?" The question was put to Peter. The question is put to us. Can you not watch one hour? Can you not stay alert to the demands of the Christian life? In accepting the way of the Christian as our way, we are aware of the obligations we assume and the special requirements that are set upon us. We are called to be responsive to God's will and to seek to express the spirit of Christ in all that we do and say. There are always other demands made upon us and other claims for our loyalty, and it is easy for us to let the responsibilities assumed when we entered the Christian life fade into the margins of our awareness.

Can you not watch one hour? Can you not stay alert to the ways in which to express your Christian commitment? As Christians we do seek to do the will of God, to express that will through our lives as we go about the business of living. It takes a full measure of imagination and sensivity to discern how we can be faithful to our commitment to God in our daily work, in our dealings with other people, in our life in the family. In our preoccupation with all the other interests and compelling concerns that compete for our attention, we may fail to stay alert to the ways in which we can actually do God's will as we go about our daily round.

Can you not watch one hour? Can you not stay alert to the needs of persons to whom you can minister in Christian love? The hand of a beggar or the insistent appeal of a panhandler may force itself to our attention so that we have to make an effort even to ignore the need that is there before us. But most often the needs of people can be easily hidden. It doesn't require great effort not to know that there are hungry children in the world. We can go through our days with the assumption that because we have enough and we are being cared for, everything must be all right for everybody. We can be oblivious to the urgent needs of the human beings with whom we share this earth, and not know the hunger and pain that others experience. All too easily we can sleep through the torments of others.

Can you not watch one hour? Can you not stay alert to the need for discipline and prayer in your relationship with God? Jesus asked the disciples to watch and to pray with him, but they fell asleep. No relationship is sustained and deepened unless there is energy expended in listening to the other, in trying to understand the other, in sharing our thoughts and dreams with the other. To pay attention to the presence of God in our lives requires the investment of ourselves in seeking to know God. Yet the days go by, we discover, without our praying and without our taking the time to reflect on the ways of God in our world and in our lives.

The apostle Paul talks about the need for sustained and steady attention as he writes to the Christians at Rome. "Never flag in zeal, be aglow with the Spirit, serve the Lord. Rejoice in your hope, be patient in tribulation, be constant in prayer" (Rom. 12:11). Zeal, patience, and constancy are important in the life of the Christian. Surely the question of Jesus presses us: "Could you not watch one hour?"

Why did Peter and the others have trouble staying awake? Why do we have trouble staying alert to the possibilities in the Christian life? Some of the dynamics in what enables us to go to sleep or in what keeps us awake can be identified. First, there is the blindness to the torment and anguish of others. Jesus had repeatedly told his disciples what he faced in Jerusalem. They knew that his enemies were there and that they would seek his life. He had eaten a final meal with them, and in the midst of the meal had warned that one of them would betray him. He had told them that they would all desert him because of what was going to happen to him that night. He had taken Peter and James and John apart and told them: "My soul is very sorrowful, even to death; remain here, and watch with me." In spite of all that, Peter and the others went to sleep. We don't go to sleep when we are truly involved with another, when we are genuinely fearful of what is coming, when we share deeply in the anguish of another. Surely Peter was concerned about Jesus and what might happen to him, but not that concerned. Surely Peter knew the threats that Jesus faced, but he hadn't let the full impact of what might happen hit.

When Jesus asks why we cannot watch one hour, he is asking whether we are really concerned about the hurts of our world and its people. Don't we really care for the children whose lives are stunted and twisted because they don't have enough to eat? They are children just like our children, and doesn't it matter to us that they suffer and die? Don't we really care that lonely and elderly people sit day after day with no one to take any interest in them? Don't we really care that ghetto young people cannot find a job and have no hope of finding meaningful work? When we do not watch with diligence and do not stay alert, it is in some measure because we do not care what happens to people. We do not sleep when we are deeply and passionately involved. The words of Miriam Teichner speak to our need:

> God—let me be aware.
> Stab my soul fiercely with others' pain.
> Let me walk seeing honor and stain.
> Let my hands, groping, find other hands,
> Give me the heart that divines, understands,
> Give me the courage, wounded,to fight.
> Flood me with knowledge, drench me in light.
> Please—keep me eager just to do my share
> God—let me be aware.[4]

51

"Could you not watch one hour?"

Second, we may have trouble staying awake because we are oblivious to the threats to ourselves. Not only do we not care what is happening to others, but we don't know what is happening to us. When Jesus came back the first time and found the disciples sleeping, he said to Peter: "So, could you not watch with me one hour? Watch and pray that you may not enter into temptation; the spirit indeed is willing, but the flesh is weak." Not only was Peter not aware of what Jesus was facing; he was not aware of what he was going to confront. Any followers of Jesus would be in danger when Jesus was arrested and would be tempted to deny the Lord, to sell out his convictions, to cave in to the pressures. But Peter slept on, and when the test came he failed it.

The question of Jesus: Can you not watch one hour, can you not stay alert, don't you know how you will be tempted? Who knows when the moment will come when we will be tempted to compromise our Christian convictions, to act in such a way as to deny the confession of faith we have made in Jesus Christ as Lord? There are great pressures on all of us to accede to the ways of those who get on in the world by taking bribes, or falsifying information, or hiding the truth. Who knows when the moment will come when we will be tempted to manipulate other people to our own ends, to take advantage of their weakness or gullibility? We can so easily treat people as objects whose value is measured only by their economic productivity or by their usefulness to us. Who knows when the moment will come when we are tempted to keep silent in the face of injustice? It is just too much of a hassle to fight for open housing in our community, or to oppose the misinterpretations of the welfare system, or to get into the struggle for equal and adequate educational facilities for all children. Who knows when the moment will come when we will be tempted to violate the integrity of our lives we want to uphold.

For all of us there are serious tests of our Christian convictions. It is not easy in our day, as it has not been easy in any day, to live out the commitments we have made to Jesus Christ. How can we uphold those convictions and live out those commitments unless we are alert in our awareness of the danger, and constant in our prayer and preparation for the time of testing? "Could you not watch one hour?"

Third, we may have trouble staying awake because we fail to see the significance of the tasks, often rather mundane, which are now given us to do. Just before going to Gethsemane, Jesus had warned his disciples that they would all leave him. "Peter declared to him, 'Though they all fall away because of you, I will never fall away.' Jesus said to him, 'Truly, I say to you, this very night, before the cock crows, you will deny me three times.' Peter said to him, 'Even if I must die with you, I will not deny you'" (Matt. 26:33-35). Peter thought that he was prepared to die for the Lord, but that wasn't what Jesus was asking of him at that moment. Jesus asked him to watch and pray with him for one hour, and Peter wasn't up to that. There is no need to be cynical about Peter's pledge that he would die with his Lord. Surely Peter believed honestly that he would be willing to lay down his life for his Lord. But that was something off in a hazy future when the noble deed is surrounded by a rosy glow, and the ultimate sacrifice is given with grace and nobility. Staying awake for an hour was the thing that needed to be done now, and Peter wasn't up to that.

There is a bit of Peter in most of us. We dream of the noble, heroic, and great things we will do; and we can picture ourselves making any sacrifice demanded. But our picture of that moment of triumphant sacrifice tends to be a bit romantic, without the fear and hatred and pain, leaving only the noble deed. Or we set our sights on the big things but fail to stay alert for the "little" things. The "little" things we think we can easily do. So we set out to create the perfect marriage but make a big issue about taking the garbage out. We set out to make the world more Christian, but haven't time to help in a community activity for underprivileged children. Edith Wharton wrote of one of her characters in *The House of Mirth:* "If Lily was faintly aware of fresh difficulties ahead, she was sure of her ability to meet them: it was characteristic of her to feel that the only problems she could not solve were those with which she was familiar."[5] "Could you not watch one hour?" Can you not do the thing that is now before you to do?

Finally, we may have trouble staying awake because we are not geared up for the sustained effort. Peter was tired. It had been a long day. Now that the night had come he was not prepared to make the effort to stay awake. We get tired in our efforts to be faithful. The struggle to get the rights to which all persons are entitled goes slowly and is often discouraging. We went on our marches and mounted our campaigns, and we thought that would do the job. And we're tired and don't feel like taking on the struggle to obtain economic and social opportunities for minority persons. Maturing as a Christian takes thought and effort and prayer. We may have begun our Christian pilgrimage with a great burst of enthusiasm, but it takes a lifetime of listening and praying, and sometimes we get tired. We've worked a long time in the church and done many jobs, and when they come to ask us to do one more, we are tired.

"Could you not watch one hour?" Can we sustain the discipline and the effort required to be faithful? Sir Francis Drake wrote this prayer: "O Lord God, when Thou givest to Thy servants to endeavor any great matter, grant us to know that it is not the beginning but the continuing of the same until it is thoroughly finished which yieldeth the true glory." Or there is the prayer of G. K. Chesterton in the words of a hymn which might serve us this day: "From sleep, and from damnation, deliver us, good Lord."[6]

8

How Can You Say?

The Question of Jesus
"He who has seen me has seen the Father; how can you say, 'Show us the Father'?" (John 14:9).

Almost anything that goes wrong in human affairs can be traced to a breakdown in communication. Even with the "almost" at the beginning of the sentence, that may be a slightly exaggerated statement. But it is notable how often problems arise because of a failure to communicate. Two 747s collided as they were both trying to take off from a fog-shrouded airport, apparently because the pilot of one of the planes failed to understand the instructions from the tower. No matter who sits in the White House, there seems to be a steady flow of complaint from members of Congress that they are not consulted enough or informed sufficiently—complaint that phone calls are not answered, complaint that advance information is not given before public announcement is made, complaint that impact on specific constituencies of particular policies is not adequately considered. Companies institute new policies and run into stiff resistance from their workers, not primarily because of the substance of the policies but because the workers were not informed that there were going to be changes and helped to understand what the changes mean.

In interpersonal relationships, the need for communication is evident. Much of the work of marriage counselors is helping husbands and wives learn how to communicate with each other. The problems of communication between parents and children are notable. Friendships can be sustained only when people have the capacity to communicate with each other. Communication involves both the capacity to articulate and to listen, to speak and to hear. A failure of communication can come from either side. There may be a breakdown because a person fails to express what he or she wants to make known, or because a person fails to hear or perceive what is being said.

There are enormous resources and sophisticated instruments of communication available in our time. Certainly the speed and complexity of our means of communication is one of the defining conditions of our age when we compare our time with earlier periods of human history. In the day of the pony express on the American frontier, it would take days at best for word of something that happened on the East Coast to reach the frontier. In our time, through satellite communication, events on the other side of the world are brought into our homes even as they happen. The means of communication are many and varied—television, radio, telephone, magazines, newspapers, books, records, duplicating machines, tape recorders, movies, slide transparencies, computers, letters. And we have become quite aware of the importance of interpersonal communication, and have people who have developed skills in facilitating the ability of people to interact.

But there are still problems and failures. There are still disasters because people didn't communicate with one another. With all of the resources and awareness that we have, why are there still problems? Why do people fail to communicate? A number of reasons can be noted. For one thing, there are times when people fail to communicate because of simple oversight. They forget about some people who need to be informed about a decision or a policy before it is implemented. They get so caught up in getting a job done that they don't take the time to consider all of the people who have a legitimate interest in what is going on.

A second reason people fail to communicate is that they have become alienated from one another. When a country breaks diplomatic relations with another nation, the problem of keeping in touch obviously becomes more difficult. People who are so angry with one another that they won't speak have obviously raised serious barriers to communication. People who have dismissed others as inferior or worthless will clearly have a problem in communicating with them. If people don't care about one another, the channels of communication are difficult to maintain.

A third reason people fail to communicate has to do with the complexity of what is to be communicated. Anyone working on the frontier of any field of knowledge will have difficulty both in articulating the insights for which he or she is grasping, and in putting the insights into words and concepts that can be understood by others. Communication between two human beings is never perfect, because people are infinitely complex. No one can adequately articulate what is being felt or thought or experienced. No one can grasp completely what another is feeling or thinking or experiencing. The complexity of a single human being inevitably makes communicating partial and difficult.

Yet a fourth reason why people fail to communicate is that they lack a common medium. The most obvious example is the limitation on communication when people do not share a common language. When the words and signs and symbols do not have a common meaning, people are largely cut off from one another. Less severe but nonetheless real is the problem of communication between the generations. Each generation develops its own "in" language, which is used both to intensify the sharing between peers and to cut off the possibility of understanding by people both older and younger.

A fifth reason why people fail to communicate is because the receiver is faulty. No matter how good the signal being sent, if the receiver cannot or will not take the signal, nothing will come across. Or to put it in other terms, when people don't listen, they can't hear. When people don't pay attention, they can't understand. No matter how clearly the word is spoken, if people aren't interested in what is being said, they won't hear. No matter how clearly the word is spoken, if people are distracted by other concerns, they won't hear.

Chester Pennington wrote a book with the intriguing title *God Has a Communication Problem.* I suppose we usually think of God as not having any problems. But Pennington describes God's communication problem in this way: "A sensitive reading of Scripture certainly indicates that God has a communication problem. The scriptural account of his dealings with us suggests that he has 'one earth of a time' communicating his message, even to his chosen people. Again and again he says to them [us], 'This is what I want you to do.' Just as often they [we] reply, 'We know well enough what you want us to do, but we'd like to try our own way.' He warns, 'You're liable to destroy yourselves.' And they [we] respond, 'We'll take our chances.' And they did [we do] with recorded results—usually disastrous."[7]

Beginning with the fourteenth chapter of the Gospel of John, there is an extended account of the conversation Jesus had with his disciples in the hours just before he was arrested and brought to trial. Jesus had been with his disciples now for a considerable period. They had seen his deeds; they had heard his words; they had shared his life. So one might suppose that he felt some confidence in these last hours that they could understand what he was saying. But it becomes clear that Jesus had a serious communication problem. For example, right at the beginning of his conversation with the disciples he says to them, "And you know the way where I am going." Thomas immediately destroyed any confidence Jesus might have had that they understood him, for Thomas said to him, "Lord, we do not know where you are going; how can we know the way?"

Then Jesus talked about how the disciples had come to know the Father. Philip squashed any confidence Jesus might have had about how successful he had been, for Philip said to him, "Lord, show us the Father, and we shall be satisfied."

So it must have been with some despair that Jesus dealt with his disciples in this situation. They had been with him so long. There was so little time left for him to be with them. One senses the anguish as Jesus said to Philip: "Have I been with you so long, and yet you do not know me, Philip? He who has seen me has seen the Father; how can you say, 'Show us the Father'?"

Even in Jesus Christ it seems that God has a communication problem, for the disciples are not getting in on who Jesus is or what he is saying. Why is there a problem in God's communication with persons, with us? Why can't God or why doesn't God get through to us?

Is it a matter of oversight? Does God just forget to clue us in on what is going on?

Is it a matter of alienation or rejection? Is God just tired of us? Is the failure to communicate a way of saying that God doesn't give a damn anymore about people or what happens to them?

Is it a matter of complexity and difficulty of what is being communicated? How does the God of infinite wonder and complexity become known to people who have limited capacity to grasp and to understand?

Is it a matter of no medium of communication? How does the infinite God get through to finite people? How does the God of Spirit get through to earthly, material beings? How does the

58

eternal God get through to mortal people?

Is it a matter of lack of attention? Is there a problem because the people God seeks to reach won't pay attention, won't make the effort and commitment necessary to understand?

In his conversation with his disciples, Jesus seems to have been dismayed by their lack of understanding. "Have I been with you so long, and yet you do not know me, Philip?" From what Jesus says in this passage, it seems evident that he really expected that the disciples could understand; he really thought that they should understand. But the situation looked different from the point of view of the disciples. When Jesus said to Thomas that he knew the way where Jesus was going, Thomas immediately replied: "Lord, we do not know where you are going; how can we know the way?" (John 14:5). When Philip got into the conversation it was with the request: "Lord, show us the Father, and we shall be satisfied" (John 14:8). The disciples wanted some help. Lord, why don't you tell us where you are going before you talk about the way to get there. Lord, can't you just make things clear. You keep talking about the Father and calling us to be faithful. Just show us this God. That's all we ask. We'll be satisfied with that.

Most of us resonate with the requests of Philip and Thomas. If God has a communication problem, why doesn't God do something about it? Why doesn't God make things clear? Why doesn't God give a clear and unmistakable demonstration of divine reality? We can understand Woody Allen's lament: "If only God would give me some clear sign. Like making a large deposit in my name at a Swiss bank." Boris Grushenko in Allen's *Love and Death* keeps yearning for a clear signal that God really exists. "If he would speak just once—if he would just cough." At one point Boris tells Sonya: "If I could just see a miracle. Just one miracle. If I could see a burning bush or the seas part or my Uncle Sasha pick up a check."

To many of us there does seem to be a communication problem between God and us. When Jesus asks, "How can you say, 'Show us the Father'?" we along with the disciples have to reply that somehow we are not satisfied with what we have seen and heard and known of God. Where is the problem? It is a matter of God's oversight, of God's forgetting to clue us in? No, we had best set aside that interpretation of our situation, and not spend our time berating God for forgetting about us or failing to let us in on what is going on.

Is it then a matter of God's being so alienated from us that there is no interest or desire to communicate with the human family any longer? Again, we had best set aside that interpretation also and not spend our time feeling isolated because we think that God has turned away from us.

Is it a matter of the complexity and difficulty of what is being communicated? Yes, surely that is part of the problem. How does the infinite communicate with the finite? How does the richness of God become manifest in such a way that we can grasp it? How is the meaning of absolute truth and goodness expressed in our world that knows only partial truth and partial goodness? So we must acknowledge that we will never know God in all of the glory and splendor as the divine Being. We will never know the perfection of goodness which is in God. We will never lay hold on the absolute, the final, the unchanging, the ultimate Truth. To ask to know God in perfection and fullness is to ask to know more than the limitation of human existence allows. To demand that God give complete and unmistakable evidence is to demand what cannot be given. Suppose that we did demand that God work a miracle to establish beyond doubt the divine reality, and suppose that God granted that demand. Whatever form the miracle took would be suspect for us, and there would always be the question whether what had happened was genuinely the action of God. We can always find another interpretation of the burning bush, or the parting seas, or Uncle Sasha picking up the check. So God does indeed have a communication problem in making the finite aware of the infinite, in making the limited aware of the unlimited, in making persons caught in their mortality aware of the eternal dimension of their life.

What about the problem God has in finding the medium of communication with us? When Philip said to Jesus, "Lord, show us the Father, and we shall be satisfied," Jesus made a direct response. "Jesus said to him, 'Have I been with you so long, and yet you do not know me, Philip? He who has seen me has seen the Father; how can you say, "Show us the Father"?'" (John 14:9). God has found the medium of communication with us. God became a person to come to us in Jesus Christ. People have properly found hints and clues about God in various situations and events and realities of their common life. The fact that the world exists at all points for some to a Creator. The movements of history point for some to the God who controls the destiny of humanity on this earth. The immediate sense of the presence of God points for some to the divine reality. All of these are meaningful and appropriate ways to seek for God's communication with us. But Jesus points us to himself as the supreme medium God uses to communicate. "He who has seen me has seen the Father . . . The words that I say to you I do not speak on my own authority; but the Father who dwells in me does his works. Believe me that I am in the Father and the Father in me" (v. 10).

God chose to communicate with us through Jesus Christ. In Christ we see God's endless love and care for us. In Christ we know both the judgment and the mercy of God upon us. In Christ we discern the real power of God, the power of love which suffers on our behalf, even to death on a cross. In Christ we discern the eternal triumph of life over death as God raised him from the dead. In Christ we glimpse the fulfillment of the purpose God ordains for human life in giving and serving. In Christ we glimpse the presence of the kingdom of God now in our midst, and we experience the promise and hope of the full realization of that Kingdom. God has found the medium of communication with us. "He who has seen me has seen the Father."

The question of Jesus to Philip is surely his question to us: "How can you say, 'Show us the Father'?" That question points directly to the final problem of communication we have mentioned. There can be no communication if the listener does not hear or the looker does not see. There can be no communication if the one who experiences does not discern and appropriate what is happening. "Have I been with you so long, and yet you do not know me, Philip?" If God is to communicate with us, then we have to listen with sensitivity; we have to be discerning of who Jesus is; we have to be able to grasp something of what his presence with us means; we have to be willing to heed what is being said to us.

The question of Jesus to Philip is on target, and is the question to us. "How can you say, 'Show us the Father'?" For, "He who has seen me has seen the Father."

9

Why Do You Call Me Good?

The Question of Jesus
"And Jesus said to him, 'Why do you call me good? No one is good but God alone'" (Mark 10:18).

The floor of the Senate of the Congress of the United States is a place where florid prose can frequently be heard. Senators seem to be given to a ritualistic style and extravagant statement. There is constant referral to "the distinguished Senator from the great state of. . . ." There was an occasion several years ago when the prose heard in that place was exceedingly extravagant, even for that setting. The occasion came on the day when Hubert Humphrey came to the Senate for what people knew to be the last time. He was in the midst of his struggle with cancer but found the strength to come back to that place he loved dearly in order to receive the tribute of his colleagues. There was speech after speech extolling his virtues in the kind of exalted language which seems to resound in that place. Finally the last speech was made, and the time came for Mr. Humphrey to respond. He began by saying: "My good friend, Dale Bumpers, just leaned across the aisle and said, 'This is a little too much, isn't it Hubert?' And I said, 'Hush, I like it.'"

There are certainly appropriate occasions for extolling the virtues of people. Hubert Humphrey's return to the Senate in the midst of his struggle with cancer was one of them. People are and should be recognized at the time of retirement. They are recognized after they have been in a position for twenty-five or thirty or thirty-five or forty years. They are recognized if they have completed some significant task. It must be said that all too often the words of appreciation and gratitude are spoken only as a person's life is recalled at the time of his or her death. Surely it is good to give people recognition while they are still alive. Surely it is good to affirm the accomplishments for which people have labored long. Surely it is good to celebrate the contribution that people have made. Surely it is right to affirm the goodness that people have embodied and expressed in their speaking, their acting, and their being.

In the newspaper accounts of Humbert Humphrey's response to all the plaudits of the Senate, there was one word that brought grace and perspective into the situation. Humphrey told the Senate about his exchange with Senator Bumpers. The papers who reported what Humphrey said to the Senate noted that he reported his comment to Bumpers with a grin. Fortunately Mr. Humphrey didn't take it too seriously, even as he liked and appreciated and enjoyed the flowery praise. But he grinned about it, and that was the saving grace.

We do need to celebrate the goodness in people. We do need to affirm the virtues people exemplify. We do need to praise the achievements of people. But every person in Hubert Humphrey's position that day in the Senate, every person whose goodness and virtues and achievements are being praised is compelled in honesty to ask the question that Jesus put to a man who had once come to him. The man addressed Jesus as "good teacher." The man asked Jesus a profound question: "What must I do to inherit eternal life?" Before Jesus answered the question, he reacted to the way in which the man had addressed him. The man had called him "good teacher," and Jesus immediately asked: "Why do you call me good?"

Why do you call me good? It is a question all of us must ask if others ever begin to note our virtues and praise our accomplishments. Why do you call me good? No matter how much I have given for others, don't you know the greed which has tempted me to grasp for more? Why do you call me good? No matter how much I have tried to reach out to others, don't you know the arrogance of spirit which has tempted me to look down on people who have less education, lower prestige, fewer resources? Why do you call me good? No matter how much I have seemed to care for others, don't you know the pride which has tempted me to want to be sure that I got due credit for the help I gave? Why do you call me good? No matter how much I have rejoiced in the accomplishments of others, don't you know the envy and jealousy which have tinged my spirit? Why do you call me good? No matter how virtuous I have appeared in public, don't you know I have been sorely tempted to take advantage of others when I could do it without anyone knowing? Why do you call me good? No matter what I have been, don't you know the many ways in which I have distorted and corrupted what I ought to be?

Surely we should celebrate the goodness in persons and exalt their virtues. But there is a saving grace when such plaudits can be met with a grin. There is a saving grace when extravagant praise is put in the perspective of honest assessment of ourselves, our limitations and corruptions. Why do you call me good? That is an appropriate question for us to ask, a question that recognizes that while there are good qualities in all of us, there are also distortions of life and spirit within all of us.

Jesus asks the question, "Why do you call me good?" When the question comes from him, it comes with different meaning and significance. When the question comes from Jesus, we respond in a different way. If another person asks us why we call him or her good, we can point to virtues. But we dare not invest that person with total goodness. We dare not define the good in terms of what that person is. No human being is so good that he or she can serve as the definition of what goodness is.

When Jesus asks, "Why do you call me good?" we dare to affirm that we call him good because he is good, because his life defines for us what goodness in human existence is. Without reservation and without ambiguity, we are moved to declare that Jesus is the complete embodiment of goodness in our world. If Jesus asks us why we call him good, we are quite prepared to speak. We call you good because of your selflessness, your ability to give yourself for others, your willingness to sacrifice even your life on a cross on behalf of others. We call you good because of your sensitivity to the needs of others, your capacity to discern what others are feeling and needing, your ability to hear what others are saying to you. We call you good because of your compassion, which leads you to enter into the joy and sorrow others are experiencing. We call you good because of your absolute loyalty to God whose will you sought to do in every word and deed of your life. We call you good because of your faithfulness in fulfilling the work God gave you to do—making known God's love and bringing God's forgiveness to all the people of this earth. We call you good because we sense in you an integrity and

64

wholeness of life, a clear sense of identity. We call you good because your life radiates a fullness of joy and peace. We call you good because we find in you the completion of love—love for God, love for others, love for yourself. If Jesus asks us, "Why do you call me good?" we can surely tell him.

In the scripture, Jesus asks this question of a man who had addressed him as good teacher. When Jesus asks this man why he calls Jesus good, he is not looking for an answer. He is not asking the man to list his virtues. He is not asking the man to praise him for his good works. For even Jesus does not claim goodness as an achievement of his efforts. Even Jesus does not point to himself as the source of goodness. Jesus asks the man: "Why do you call me good? No one is good but God alone." Jesus does not deny his own goodness, but points to God as the ultimate Good, as the source of all goodness, including his own. When Jesus asks us why we call him good, he is not inviting us to list all of the attributes of his life that we discern, attributes such as we have noted above. When Jesus asks us, he directs us beyond the quality and character of his life to the source of all goodness. "Why do you call me good? No one is good but God alone."

To say that God alone is good is to affirm that no human formulation of the good is absolute and final. We try to define the good, and that is helpful, but no definition is exhaustive and complete. In our human efforts to describe and interpret the good, we can reach toward what we mean by the good, but no human definition is absolute. We try to draw up rules of right and wrong, and that is helpful, but no set of commandments fully captures the meaning of the good. The good is not fully defined by the Boy Scout laws, by the Golden Rule, by the Ten Commandments. The goodness of God is beyond all rules.

The man who asked Jesus what he must do to inherit eternal life is reminded by Jesus about the commandments. Jesus says to him: "You know the commandments: 'Do not kill, Do not commit adultery, Do not steal, Do not bear false witness, Do not defraud, Honor your father and mother.'" The man responds that he has kept all of these commandments from his youth. Obviously he was a good man, better than most of us. But he had come to ask Jesus about inheriting eternal life, coming to Jesus out of a sense of need for something more than keeping a set of rules. "And Jesus looking upon him loved him, and said to him, 'You lack one thing; go, sell all that you have, and give it to the poor, and you will have treasure in heaven; and come follow

65

me'" (Mark 10:21). The word of Jesus to this man is not to be taken as one more commandment he has to keep in order to reach the fulfillment of life. Perfect goodness is not found by giving away everything we have, extreme as that commandment sounds. Rather, Jesus is saying to the man that the goodness of life, that eternal life, is not reached by following any set of rules. Only God is good, and our goodness does not earn us eternal life. Only God is good, and we enter into the life eternal when we accept that goodness as we seek to follow Jesus Christ.

Trying to define the good is helpful, and seeking the laws that guide us toward the good is helpful, but we are most helped to understand the good and strive toward the good as we discern the good embodied in other people. It is a good person who helps us to understand what it means to be good in our world. It is a good person who inspires us to strive in our own living to express the good. But the assertion of Jesus warns us once again not to invest too much in the goodness of others. "No one is good but God alone." We can rejoice in the goodness of others; we can be helped by the goodness of others; we can be inspired by the goodness of others. But we dare not count too much on the goodness of others. For all of us share the frailties and limitations of human existence. Though there is certainly goodness in other persons, we need to remember the admonition of Jesus that no one is good but God alone.

To say that God alone is good is to affirm that God is good. At the heart of reality is goodness. That assertion is not always easy to make. There is much in our world that is evil and destructive and hurtful.

A tornado sweeps down on a community and in seconds destroys a row of homes and kills six people.

Torture continues to be used as a means of civil repression.

A woman is raped on a pool table while patrons of the bar cheer on her assailants.

A child dies of leukemia.

A drunk driver runs head-on into a car, and kills a husband and wife and three children.

A minority group is denied political, civil, economic, and personal rights that are claimed by the majority.

Hundreds of thousands of refugees wander the face of the earth because they have been driven from their land.

Millions of Jews were slaughtered in the Holocaust.

The reality of evil and sin in our world cannot be doubted. In our pessimistic moments it is easy to believe that all is corrupt, that nothing will endure, that no one's life finally counts. Jesus was certainly not blind to the reality of evil in this world. He looked at the city of Jerusalem and wept for it. He encountered in his ministry the full measure of spite and hate. He reckoned long before the end that his course would bring him to the ultimate penalty his enemies could inflict upon him, even his execution as a criminal. But Jesus never wavered in his conviction about the goodness of God. "No one is good but God alone." He believed in the goodness of God. He found hope in the goodness of God. He trusted in the goodness of God. So we dare to affirm that reality is not finally perverse and corrupt and destructive. In spite of all the evidence, we believe that there is good in our world because we can share the conviction of Jesus that only God is good.

Finally, to say that God alone is good is to see the goodness in Jesus Christ as an expression of the goodness of God. Jesus does not make claims for his own insights or his own virtues. Jesus does not draw attention to himself, but always points beyond himself. Jesus embodies goodness as he manifests the goodness of the will and character of God. Jesus asks, "Why do you call me good?" We make a bold affirmation when we call him good. For we declare that in this person is the meaning of the goodness of God in our world. When we want to know what the good is, we look to Jesus Christ. He doesn't solve all our dilemmas about the good. He doesn't give us easy answers about what the good is in every situation. But when we seek to know what goodness is in our world, we look to him. We do come to understand goodness and to long for goodness through seeing it in others—a parent, a friend, a trusted advisor, a modern-day saint. But above all, we understand goodness by seeing it in Jesus Christ.

So we answer the question of Jesus, "Why do you call me good?" We call you good because in you we see the goodness of God in the midst of our life.

10

Do You Believe?

The Question of Jesus
"And Jesus said to them, 'Do you believe that I am able to do this?'" (Matt. 9:28).

It's safe to say that computers are a mixed blessing. The modern world couldn't function without them. They are great for keeping track of vast numbers. They do in seconds computations that would take people years to do. Increasingly we are dependent on the computer for everything from scheduling classes in the high school to navigating 747 flights, from figuring the gross national product to tracking the inventory in a supermarket. Life as we know it today wouldn't be possible without computers. But they are a mixed blessing, for if a human being ever gets fouled up in the computer, it's a disaster. To get things straightened out if we have been billed for something we didn't buy is almost a hopeless cause. To get a wrong entry into the computer at the bank can have serious consequences indeed.

To try to communicate with the computer by the standard means of communication between people can result in a high level of frustration. It seems to be futile to write letters to a computer complaining that the item on the bill was not purchased by us. After a series of such letters without results, we may be reduced to taking an ice pick to those cards which sternly admonish us not to fold, spindle, or mutilate, in the hope that if enough holes are punched in the card the computer will blow a fuse and somebody will pay attention. For it seems that the computer will grind out the bills endlessly, each succeeding one with more dire threats about what will happen if we don't pay up promptly.

The dire threats are all too real, for a mistake in the computer can have awful consequences for a credit rating. A black mark in the computer, or whatever the computer's version of a black mark may be, and we are branded for life as a poor risk. To be branded as a poor credit risk is not a condition to be contemplated nonchalantly. The modern world functions not only with computers but on credit, and if we don't have the credit we don't function very well.

There is a broader issue than just a person's credit rating, and that is the issue of a person's credibility. A good credit rating is one way in which a person establishes credibility, of course. A good credit rating is witness that if money is loaned or goods sold to us, the promise to pay will be honored. Responsible action in repaying what we owe is one factor in our credibility, but there are others. If we say that a product we are selling is of a certain quality, are we speaking accurately? If we say that we will do something, do we follow through whether it is convenient or not? If we say that something happened, will subsequent investigation establish that the events did occur as we said they did? If we are asked for our opinion on an issue, are we willing to give an honest answer? When people deal with us, do they have the sense that they know where we are and what we are thinking and what we are intending?

The issue of credibility has become signficant in our common life in recent years. Watergate and the related incidents cast serious doubt on the credibility of government. The public disclosure of the payoffs and bribes by some of the major corporations in this country have cast doubt on the credibility of business. Reports issued from Vietnam of what was happening during the war there cast doubt on the credibility of the military. Evidence of unnecessary surgery has cast doubt on the credibility of the medical profession. The general image of used car salespeople may be quite unfair to many persons in the business, but the great possibility of misrepresentation and fraud has created a sense in some people that used car salespersons are not to be trusted.

A Gallup Poll sometime ago asked people what kind of confidence they had in the church. Only 44 percent said that they had a great deal of confidence in the church and in its leadership. At first reading that doesn't sound very good. It is cause for deep regret that fewer than half the people surveyed expressed strong conviction in the reliability of the church. But the picture of how people feel about the church is somewhat altered when it becomes part of the total picture of how people feel about other institutions of American life. The percentage of people who said they had great confidence in various institutions is as follows:

The military	27%
Public schools	22%
The Presidency	23%
The Supreme Court	22%
Congress	14%
Labor unions	12%
Big business	10%

It is more encouraging for the church to have 44 percent of the people expressing great confidence in the light of these other figures, but the low credibility of many of our public institutions is cause for concern. A society is strong and stable only when people have confidence in each other and in the institutions that enable the common life to function.

In both personal relations and institutional structures, the issue of credibility is crucial. We can relate deeply and meaningfully to persons only if we trust them; others can hear and accept what we offer only when they trust us. We can learn from others only if we trust them; others can accept our insights and understandings only if they trust us. We can cooperate with others only if we trust them; others will accept our offers to work with them only if they trust us. We can accept help from others only if we trust them; others will receive what we have to offer them only if they trust us. The health of our personal relationships depends upon the mutual trust we have.

Not only in personal relationships, but also in the broader social structures, the issue of credibility is crucial. In a free society, the power of the government rests finally on the consent of the governed, and the governed will give their consent only if they sense the basic trustworthiness in those to whom power is entrusted. The founders of this nation knew well the corruptibility of every person, and they sought to build such a system of checks and balances so that persons in authority would be accountable and limited. The system is strengthened when the people perceive both that those in authority are to be trusted and that they are being held accountable for what they do in office. The system is weakened when the people sense that the safeguards of the system are failing to insure that those who hold the public trust are indeed worthy of that trust.

What is true of political institutions is true of institutions in every area of our common life. If we no longer trust the automobile manufacturer to produce a good car or to stand behind the warranty of the car, we will turn to another make. If we no longer believe that the doctor is prescribing solely out of concern for our well-being but in part out of intent to enrich himself or herself, we will seek elsewhere for medical care. The public schools of a community are in profound trouble when they no longer have the confidence of the people whose children are being educated there.

All of us are dependent in many ways on the credibility of others. There are circumstances when we can establish for ourselves what the facts are; when we can assess for ourselves what the truth is; when we have sufficient knowledge to know what the situation is. When we have the ability to make our own determination, we are not so dependent on the credibility of others. But in the midst of the complexity of life, we are very limited in our capacity to make our own determination about the facts or the truth. This is the age of the specialist, the age of the expert. A person can be an expert only in very limited areas; outside of those areas the person must depend on the credibility of others. The plumber will know how much work actually needs to be done in repairing the heating system but must trust the surgeon to make the decision about an operation. The surgeon will know whether the operation is necessary but must trust the plumber when the radiators don't work.

How do we establish our own credibility, or how do we gain confidence in the credibility of others? Credibility is established primarily when a person's words or promises are authenticated by actions. If a person selling a used car says that the car is in good condition and subsequent performance proves that the car does run well, the credibility of the person is enhanced. If a person takes goods on credit and makes the payments on time, the credibility of the person is enhanced. If a person affirms the value of education and makes intensive effort to learn, the credibility of the person is enhanced. We trust the person who has been proven trustworthy. We are willing to accept a person on faith when there is evidence that the public utterance of the person accords with the private living. The longer we experience another's integrity of word and action, the more confident we become when we must depend on their credibility.

When the trust that a person has placed in others has been violated, it becomes exceedingly difficult to establish credibility with that person. In a move of great courage and hope, a family took an eight-year-old boy into their home. The boy had been abandoned by his parents and abused by the people with whom he had been placed. His experience had taught him that adults were not to be trusted. It took almost three years before the family who took him in made a breakthrough, so that he became able to trust them when they spoke and acted on their care for him. They made the breakthrough by demonstrating time and time again their care, by refusing to turn away when he lashed out in anger, by continuing to believe that they could gain his confidence. A trusting relationship between two persons depends not only on the trustworthiness of the one, but on the capacity to trust of the other.

In the religious dimensions of our lives, we enter most profoundly into the realm of faith. Theologians have debated and differed over the extent to which reason might establish the reality and the ways of God. Theologians have debated and differed over how far the experiences of this world can reveal God to us. But for the Christian, God transcends the limits of reason and expressions of the natural world. God is known and accepted in faith. Christian affirmations about God are assertions of what we believe to be true. We can talk about proof and knowledge when dealing with other people and exploring this physical world in ways we cannot talk about proof and knowledge when we declare who God is and what God has done.

We live by faith. But the faith is not totally without evidence. We have grounds for what we believe about the nature of God and the activities of God. One of the significant sources of our faith is the testimony of others about who God is for them. We learn first of God from the faith and the convictions of others. We hear in the words of others the evidence that they believe in a God who cares for them and guides them. As we grow and mature in our faith, we learn to ask of the credibility of those who speak to us of God. Can we trust what they say to us when they speak of the ways of God, of the claims of God upon us, of the appropriate response to what God asks of us? The question of the credibility of the witness is as significant in assessing religious claims as in every other area of life. There are charlatans in religion as elsewhere. There are those in religion as elsewhere who would exploit their "expertise" and our ignorance to their own ends. So we properly test the credibility of those who speak to us of God, applying much the same tests we would use elsewhere. Do their own lives reflect the commitment to the God of whom they speak? If they speak of a God of love, do they manifest love in what they do? If they speak of a God of righteousness, is there a struggle for righteousness in their own lives? If they speak of a God of forgiveness and reconciliation, do they live as forgiven people and as people who forgive others? We learn of God from others as they speak to us of God, but even more significant is the witness of those whose lives manifest the God of whom they speak.

For the Christian, there is a final and crucial witness to the truth of God. Ultimately the value and authority of our faith in God rests on the credibility of Jesus Christ. We seek to understand the ways of God, using the best gifts of mind and thought. We seek to discern the ways of God as we find evidence of God's work in the world around us. We seek to glimpse the meaning of God as we hear the testimony of those whose lives have been shaped by their faith. But it is Jesus of Nazareth who claims to manifest God in our world. Scripture makes many claims that the fullest witness to God is found in Jesus the man of Nazareth, in Jesus the Christ. Matthew describes the birth of Jesus as the fulfillment of the prophecy through Isaiah that one shall be born who shall be called Emmanuel, God with us. Paul testifies that "God was in Christ reconciling the world to himself." Particularly in the Gospel of John is there strong identification by Jesus of himself with God. "My teaching is not mine, but his who sent me; if any man's will is to do his will, he shall know whether the teaching is from God or whether I am speaking on my own authority." "I and the Father are one. He who has seen me has seen the Father." John opens his Gospel with the ringing assertion: "In the beginning was the Word, and the Word was with God, and the Word was God. . . . And the Word became flesh and dwelt among us" (John 1:1, 14).

Christian conviction about God roots basically in the credibility of Jesus Christ. Jesus makes extraordinary claims for himself, and others make extraordinary claims for him. Either he is what he claims to be, or he is an imposter. Either he speaks of what he knows, or he is a deceiver. If we believe him, we have access to profound expression of the ways of God. If we don't believe him, all that he witnessed to us about God has no validity. On several occasions Jesus asked people if they believed in him and in what he offered to do for them. After the death of Lazarus, Jesus came to the home of his sisters, Mary and Martha, and when Martha lamented the death of her brother Jesus said to her: "I am the resurrection and the life; he who believes in me, though he die, yet shall he live, and whoever lives and believes in me shall never die. Do you believe this?" (John 11:25f.). On another occasion Jesus healed a man who had been blind from birth, and later confronted the man with the question: "Do you believe in the Son of man?" On yet another occasion two blind men followed Jesus, crying to him to have mercy on them. Before doing anything for them, Jesus confronted them with the question, "Do you believe that I am able to do this?" Then there was the moment when Jesus asked his disciples what people were saying about him, and then confronted them with the question: "But who do you say that I am?"

In various ways and with different people, Jesus pressed the issue of his credibility. What do you believe? What do you believe about me? Do you believe that I can do what you ask of me? Who do you think that I am? Jesus presses the question of what we believe about him. Do we accept his credibility when he speaks and acts?

It makes a profound difference how we answer when we face the question of Jesus about whether we believe in him. If we believe in him and in who he claims to be, we can learn from him of the truth of God, or the meaning and purpose of life, or the way to eternal life. If we believe in him, we can be healed by him of the ills of the body and the ills of the spirit, for we are the blind and deaf and lame and dead. If we believe in him, we discern the presence of God in the midst of our earthly and human existence.

But is Jesus credible? Do we have grounds for accepting his claims? Is there any substantiation which would enable us to answer the question of Jesus with confident affirmation of who he is and what he can do? Or do we just take it on blind faith that Jesus is who he claims to be? There are two tests that we can apply in testing the claims of Jesus, like the tests we use in assessing the credibility of any person. First, does the life of Jesus authenticate his words? Can we sense in him an integrity of life? It can reasonably be claimed that of all people, Jesus demonstrates most fully an integration of his words and his actions. There is nothing in the record of what he said that rings false with what he did. There is nothing in what we know of him which contradicts

74

what he said of himself. He talked of trusting God, and he lived a life of trust. He talked of God's demand for forgiveness, and he forgave even those who tortured and crucified him. He talked of love for God and neighbor and self, and he loved God and neighbor and self. He talked of the importance of seeking the will of God, and he lived obedient to that will in all that he did. From all that we know about Jesus, his life authenticates his words.

Second, does Jesus deliver on his promises? We need to be clear about what Jesus promised people. He didn't call his disciples to a life of ease or comfort or wealth or success. He didn't promise them that they would live long if they followed him. He did promise wholeness and health. He did promise significant work to do. He did promise the sustaining care of God. On those promises he delivered.

If we are to relate to Jesus and learn of him and receive from him, we must answer the question of his credibility. The question of Jesus is crucial. "Do you believe that I am able to do this?"

11

What Will It Profit?

The Question of Jesus
"For what will it profit a man, if he gains the whole world and
forfeits his life?" (Matt. 16:26).

There is an ambiguity about ambition. I had a classmate in
seminary who was open about his ambitions for "success" in the
ministry. Even as a student, he had set for himself a timetable for
his life. The first church out of school had to be a church of a
certain size, larger than the churches most of his classmates
would have as a first parish. The second church that he intended
to have by age twenty-eight would have at least 500 members. By
the time he was thirty-five he intended to have a church of at least
1500 members. And by the time he was forty-five, he had on his
schedule that he would be a bishop. He had no hesitation in
letting people know of his ambitions, and as the time came to
take a position in his first church, he made it clear that he would
not consider a call to any smaller church.

Such open and brash statement of what he intended to do
drew mixed reactions from his classmates. On the one hand, there
was a certain admiration for his open aggressiveness. He was a
man who knew what he wanted and who intended to go after his
goals. There was a recogntion by many that he only stated bla-
tently the ambitions that others had but would not voice so
publicly. There are pressures on people entering the ministry to
"succeed," pressures that come from outside expectations and
from internal desires. Many of the man's classmates were as

caught up as he in striving for success as measured by bigger churches and powerful positions, and they recognized that there was an honesty in such forthright and open statement of what he wanted.

On the other hand, there was condsiderable negative response to ambition so openly declared. At the level of strategy, people question the wisdom of such blatant aggressiveness. Ministers are not supposed to be that way. A sure way for a minister to lose out on a job is to be too aggressive in seeking it. But there was a more significant unease about this man's vision of what he wanted to achieve. There was the sense that somehow he was in the wrong business, that he had missed the whole point of what the Christian ministry is all about. Ministers are not called to climb the ladder of success, as defined in terms of size or church or position of power. Ministers are called to a life of service. They must be concerned about finding the position in which their talents and and abilities can best be used and must make careful decisions about what positions they will accept. But there is a pervasive sense that the person called to the ministry should not be consumed with a passion to succeed as measured on the world's terms.

His fellow seminary students perceived rightly that the man with such open ambition was in an ambiguous situation. Yet surely it is not only the ministry in which there is ambiguity in ambition. Ambition is a positive force in the lives of persons. Their ambition pushes people to test themselves, to push to their limits, to develop their capacities. We judge it a waste when people of ability fail to develop the gifts they have because they have no ambition. Ambition is necessary for great achievement. A person without ambition in life is to be pitied.

Yet ambition can become destructive. People can be driven by their ambition until they have no time for any richness of life outside the narrow focus of their particular interest. In considering the negative meanings of ambition, the quality and significance of the goals people seek are significant factors. Some goals for which people literally give their lives are not worth what their achievement costs in terms of relationships stunted, opportunities for recreation missed, horizons of interest narrowed. But apart from judgments about the worthiness of the goal, ambition for any goal can become so consuming that life is restricted rather than enhanced. To return for a moment to the example of the minister, there was the judgment that he had failed to grasp the meaning of Christian ministry. But the minister ambitious only to serve may become so compulsive about the tasks of ministry that responsibility to family or friends or self is neglected.

To raise the issue about the ambiguous character of ambition pushes toward fundamental questions of the purpose and meaning of human existence on this earth. What are the significant goals that are worth the investment of the only life one has? What goals are worth the effort demanded to achieve them? What ambitions push people toward the realization of what life is intended to be? There are no absolute answers to such questions. There are no answers which are universally valid for every person. But these are questions with which persons must struggle as they reflect on the ways in which they are investing the days and the abilities that have been given to them.

Confronting a question of Jesus pushes us to assess the ambitions which have driven our lives, pushes us to ponder the goals worth the striving of a lifetime. The question of Jesus that prompts such reflection is this: "For what will it profit a man, if he gains the whole world and forfeits his life? Or what shall a man give in return for his life?" In Alan Paton's *Cry, the Beloved Country*, Stephan Kumalo probes the issue of his existence in these words: "Who indeed knows the secret of the earthly pilgrimage? Who knows for what we live, and struggle, and die? Who knows what keeps us living and struggling, while all things break about us? Who knows why the warm flesh of a child is such comfort, when one's own child is lost and cannot be recovered? Wise men write many books, in words too hard to understand. But this, the purpose of our lives, the end of all our struggle, is beyond all human wisdom. Oh God, my God, do not thou forsake me."[8]

People are ambitious for many things and devote their energies to achieving many different goals. No list of goals for which people have striven can be complete, but those noted below give some indication of the diversity of aspirations people have:

> To be a success.
> To gain recognition and fame.
> To exercise great power.
> To make a lot of money.
> To become wise.
> To achieve security.
> To fulfill an artistic talent.
> To provide for the children.

To make the world a better place in which to live.
To acquire material possessions.
To enjoy themselves.
To gain acceptance by the right people.
To be respected and admired.
To gain knowledge.

The list could be extended indefinitely, and all of us strive for many of the goals noted. Our energies are focused on the achievement of a variety of aims.

But facing the question Jesus asked about gaining the whole world but losing life pushes us to two considerations, one negative and the other positive. First, when Jesus asks his question we are made conscious again that people can lose the meaning of life when they are driven by the wrong ambitions and make the wrong investments. We are necessarily involved in the struggles of this world—to provide for our physical and emotional needs, to establish ourselves in our relationships with other people, to have a sense of our own self-worth, to find our place in the scheme of things. But the question of Jesus reminds us that we can gain all that the world has to offer and still forfeit life.

There is an endless variety of ways in which people can gain the world and forfeit life. A person finds self-worth in fame, and when the fickle crowd leaves, there is nothing left. A person dedicates life to the rat race to the top, and having made it finds that getting there was not worth the effort. A person scrapes and sacrifices for the prestige of a bigger house in the right neighborhood only to find that life is no more satisfying in the big house than the small house. A person is pressured into external manifestations of righteousness and finds the strain between outer appearance and inner reality intolerable. A person wins by violating every tenet of conscience and pays the price of self-hatred. A person walks with arrogant insistence that things will be done her way and becomes isolated from any genuine human relationship. A person is so eager to please that he agrees with anything and everyone, and also becomes isolated from any genuine human relationship, for he has nothing to contribute.

The question of Jesus serves to make us ask again about the meaning of the ambitions that drive us and the value of the goals that lure us. The answer to the question as Jesus puts it can be given with emphatic confidence. "What will it profit a man, if he gains the whole world and forfeits his life?" The answer: *nothing*.

Second, when Jesus asks his question, we are impelled to ask what goals do bring life. For Jesus reminds us of what we know deep down, that the achievement of this goal or that goal finally makes sense when we have some notion of The Goal, some notion of the purpose for which all of life has been given, some notion of "the why" of our existence. "What will it profit a man, if he gains the whole world and forfeits his life?" Why are we here? What is life for? What is the goal worthy of a lifetime of effort and devotion? The questions must be asked if we are to take seriously the issue raised by Jesus in his question. The questions can be asked, but as Stephen Kumalo notes, there are no easy answers. "Who indeed knows the secret of the earthly pilgrimage? Who knows for what we live, and struggle, and die?" There are no easy answers, for there is no single, precise, definitive statement that will answer the question: What is the meaning of life?

But for the Christian there is a sense of direction, a hint, a clue, a promise. We have no neat formula, but we have an example and a witness of the one who embodied life, who declared: "I came that they may have life, and have it abundantly" (John 10:10). The hint, the clue, the direction is given by Jesus just before he asks the question about what is the profit if a person gains the world and loses life. "For whoever would save his life will lose it, and whoever loses his life for my sake will find it" (Matt. 16:25).

Life is found in faithful response to God. Life is found in becoming what God intends us to become. Life is found in giving glory to God. Life is found in our relationship with God. Jesus gives us the sense of what God wants for us and wants of us. God gives us life that we may love, and in that loving find life in its fullest. In its broadest meaning, losing life for the sake of Christ means loving for the sake of Christ. There is no guide book which tells us how to love in every situation, but Jesus' embodiment of love shows us love in our world. Love shares the burden of others. Love offers forgiveness when a wrong has been done. Love gives self-worth, both to the one who loves and the one who is loved. Love gets beyond self-interest to the interests of others, beyond self-seeking to seeking the good for others. The question of Jesus forces us to consider again and again what we are doing with our lives. "What will it profit a man, if he gains the whole world and forfeits his life?" For what shall we be ambitious? For what purpose shall we use our days on this earth? How shall we find life? "For whoever would save his life will lose it, and whoever loses his life for my sake will find it" (Matt. 16:25).

80

12

Can the Wedding Guests Fast?

The Question of Jesus
"And Jesus said to them, 'Can the wedding guests fast while the bridegroom is with them?'" (Mark 2:19).

If people are looking for laughs, they don't usually head for the church. If people are in need of comedy, they head in other directions. They may try a Woody Allen movie. They may watch a situation comedy on television. They may look for a stand-up comic in a night club. The may wait for a Bob Hope special on TV. They may try a humorous play. They may buy a funny book. They may read Erma Bombeck in the local paper. But they don't usually head for the church. When people are looking for laughs they are not always successful in finding them, no matter where they look. Some situation comedies provide some laughs; others can't generate a smile even with the laughter on a sound track. Some comedians have good material and deliver it well; others strain to be funny but don't succeed. Some movies make people laugh until the tears come; others set up comedy situations that fall off the screen with a dull thud. It's not easy to find laughs in our kind of world.

Why don't people come to church when they are looking for laughs? If TV and the movies and stand-up comics can't guarantee laughter, why not try the church? People don't come to church to find humor for the good reason that the church is not designed as a place of entertainment. Preachers may be intentionally or unintentionally funny on occasion, but they are not trained to be stand-up comedians. The church is concerned with serious business, not funny business. The church has to do with religion, and religion is more often associated with the somber than with the humorous. The church is a place for prayer and meditation and thinking about God. God is not usually pictured as a comedian.

The church is concerned with the holy, not the funny. The church is concerned with sin and salvation, with hell and heaven, with judgment and mercy, which are not exactly inherently funny topics. The church is more concerned about people being good than about people having a good time. At the center of the faith professed by the church and at the center of the liturgical life of the church is a cross, an instrument of pain and anguish and death. Rather than dealing with the light and the humorous, the church talks about sacrifice and giving and obedience. The church deals with the sacred in life, and we tend to get solemn and serious when we deal with the sacred. So people tend to come to church to be serious and sober. Religious concerns deal with the fundamental issues of life, issues of meaning and destiny, issues of the good and the true. They are not laughing matters.

All of us tend to separate our religion and our humor. We don't go to the Bible for laughs. God called Moses to serious business when God laid upon him the task of leading the people of Israel out of their slavery in Egypt. God called the prophets to serious words, as when Jeremiah was told: "Behold, I have put my words in your mouth. See, I have set you this day over nations and over kingdoms, to pluck up and to break down, to destroy and to overthrow, to build and to plant" (Jer. 1:9f.). Job's struggle with God in his effort to understand the catastrophes that had befallen him was no laughing matter. There is good reason to take on a solemn and serious demeanor when we involve ourselves in the life of the church and deal with the religious issues of life.

Jesus wasn't a stand-up comedian. He didn't go around the country delivering a patter of one-liners. But Jesus didn't seem to be as serious and somber as people thought he ought to be. Jesus didn't isolate the holy into some special corner where people could deal with it with long-faced piety. The Gospels indicate that there were many complaints about Jesus and what he was doing. Many of the complaints were provoked by his willingness to share the life of ordinary people and to be involved in the mundane activities of common life. Mark describes Jesus sitting with his disciples at the table and says that there were many tax collectors and sinners sitting with them. Jesus was not only talking with these people but sharing a meal with them. When the scribes and Pharisees saw how Jesus was associating with such rowdy and irreverent people, they got upset and said to his disciples: "Why does he eat and drink with tax collectors and sinners?" In their view, Jesus' behavior wasn't proper for a religious and holy man. Matthew and Luke both report that people accused Jesus of being "a glutton and a drunkard, a friend of tax collectors and sinners."

Not only were there complaints about Jesus' behavior, but also about the disciples and what they were doing. Mark reports that the disciples of John the Baptist and the Pharisees were observing a period of fasting. Some people took their fasting as an occasion to press Jesus. "Why do John's disciples and the disciples of the Pharisees fast, but your disciples do not fast?" (Mark 2:18). These people must have thought that those who are religious should be abstemious, pure, sober, otherworldly, isolated from the corrupt of this world. They didn't approve of religious types who ate and drank with other people, who associated with sinners, who failed to observe all of the pious exercises.

Jesus had another image of the religious life, an image perhaps most clearly drawn as he responded to the question about why his disciples weren't fasting. Jesus said to them: "Can the wedding guests fast while the bridegroom is with them? As long as they have the bridegroom with them, they cannot fast" (v. 19). Jesus used the image of the wedding feast to describe life with him—a gay and joyous and exhuberant time, a time of music and laughter, a time of eating and drinking and and dancing, a time of celebrating. In describing the character of life with him, Jesus didn't use some somber, sober moment in human relationships. Rather, he said that for the disciples to be with him was like the wedding guests being with the bridegroom. "Can the wedding guests fast while the bridegroom is with them?" Obviously not!

The changing patterns and seasons of life were well described by the Preacher of Ecclesiastes. "For everything there is a season, and a time for every matter under heaven: a time to be born, and a time to die . . . a time to weep, and a time to laugh; a time to mourn, and a time to dance" (Eccl. 3:1, 2, 4). Life is not just one long laugh-in. There are profound sorrows and tragedies. There are frustrations and failures. There are moments of grave decision. There are moments of solemnity and seriousness. Jesus talks about the time of fasting. "The days will come, when the bridegroom is taken away from them, and then they will fast on that day" (Mark 2:20). Fasting and self-denial have their place in the life of the Christian and the Christian community. Fasting is a discipline of the body that can aid the discipline of the spirit. Fasting is a way of sharing the suffering of the world. Fasting is a dramatic protest in some situations. There is a time to die, a time to weep, a time to mourn, a time to fast.

But to see the church and the Christian faith and the life with Christ always in sober and somber terms is surely a mistake. "Can the wedding guests fast while the bridegroom is with them?" There are joy and celebration and laughter appropriate for the Christian and for the church. Humor is God's gift to persons, and the church with no laughter is seriously deficient. To be able to rejoice is a grace of God, and the church with no celebration has failed to grasp the full potential in the relationship of people to their God. A life or a community without profound joy have missed what Jesus Christ brought to his people.

We need to grasp the quality and the source of the joy of the Christian life. There is much humor which is rooted in the belittling of the ways of others or in the cheapening of what is holy in life. There are efforts to find joy by isolation from the ills and problems of the world, as people seek happiness by escape from the threats of nuclear war, from the realities of world hunger, from the brutalities of suffering in the midst of their own community, from the frustrations of those who are victims of prejudice. Such efforts to find laughter and joy miss the mark for the Christian. The letters of Peter were written to people who were suffering oppression and persecution, people who knew the hard cost of faithful witness. Hear what is said to people in such a situation. "By his great mercy we have been born anew to a living hope through the resurrection of Jesus Christ from the dead, and to an inheritance which is imperishable, undefiled, and unfading. . . . In this you rejoice though now you have to suffer various trials . . . without having seen him [Jesus Christ] you love him; though you do not now see him you believe in him and rejoice with unutterable and exalted joy" (1 Peter 1:3, 4, 6, 8). The sound of joy rings through these words, unutterable and exalted joy. It is not the joy of people who have isolated themselves from the anguish of others. It is not the joy of people who take satisfaction in exalting themselves over others. It is not the joy of people who have escaped

84

suffering. It is the joy of Christians.

There are laughter and joy and celebration in the Christian life and the Christian community. There is the joy of sharing life with Christ. With good reason we gather together for celebrations. We want to come together when we anticipate a joyous occasion. We come together both because joy needs to be shared and because our richest joy comes through our relationships with others. Within the Christian community we have experienced the rich pleasure when we share significant moments with others, when we know that others care for us and that we have been enabled to care for them. Basic to the joy of all of our relationships within the church is the joy of our relationship with Jesus Christ. "Can the wedding guests fast while the bridegroom is with them?" Christ is the continuing presence in our lives which enables us to rejoice and to celebrate.

There is the joy of knowing that who we are and what we do have meaning. In Christ we dare to affirm that life counts, that it is not a tale told by idiots. The words and deeds of love in our world have enduring significance. The good we are enabled to do is taken up by God and used in the mystery of the great eternal purpose. We have known the satisfaction of accomplishing some task we believe to be important for ourselves or for others. The Christian faith brings us to the joy of knowing that who we are and what we do have meaning beyond the limited goals of accomplishing this task or that job. We rejoice because we believe that the totality of who we are and what we do has meaning in the presence of the God who comes to us in Jesus Christ. There is the joy of sharing, which is given to us through Jesus. We know the joy not of escape from the world but the joy of sharing in the world. We know the joy not of grasping more and more for ourselves but the joy of giving more and more of ourselves. We have known happiness when a gift of ours has brought a blessing to another. There is laughter and celebration in the church, for through this body of Christ we are enabled to offer help to the needy, to offer food to the hungry, to offer companionship to the lonely.

Finally, there is the joy of hope. The letter of Peter described the situation of those early Christians under the threat of persecution. "By his great mercy we have been born anew to a living hope through the resurrection of Jesus Christ from the dead, and to an inheritance which is imperishable, undefiled, and unfading." We face whatever the future holds with a quiet joy, knowing of our eternal place with a loving God. Whatever people have in the present brings little joy if they live oppressed by what the future may bring, if they live fearful of what may happen to them, if they live anxious about the death that inevitably comes. For the Christian, there can be laughter and joy because there is the living hope through the resurrection of Jesus Christ.

The church is not a nightclub with a stand-up comic as the feature attraction. But the church is not a drab and dismal place where people come to endure a few moments of solemnity for the good of their souls. Jesus gave us the image of the church—the wedding feasts where there are gaity and laughter and celebration. For Jesus asked: "Can the wedding guests fast while the bridegroom is with them?"

13

Do You Want to be Healed?

The Question of Jesus
"Do you want to be healed?" (John 5:6).

Sometimes foolish questions get asked. Every evening about 10 o'clock, I ask our dog if he wants to go for a walk. That's a foolish question, for he invariably leaps to his feet and tears for the front door. After driving in the car for four hours, it is a foolish question to ask the children if they would like to stop and get something to eat. It's a foolish question to ask someone who has just won a million dollars in the lottery if he is excited. During the Olympics, a reporter interviewed the parents of the United States gymnast who had just received the first perfect score in the history of the United States' team. The reporter asked the parents if they were pleased with the score. That's a foolish question. An interviewer asked a major league pitcher who had just turned in a one-hit shutout if he was pleased with his performance. That's a foolish question. There is little point in asking questions when the answer is immediately obvious to everyone. As long as he has an ounce of energy left, I can't imagine our dog declining an invitation to go for a walk.

On one occasion Jesus appeared to ask a foolish question. It was in Jerusalem at a pool near the sheep gate. According to the tradition, when the waters of the pool were troubled, the first person to enter the water would be healed. In the five porticos around the pool lay the blind, the lame, the paralyzed. There was one man who had been ill for thirty-eight years who was lying beside the pool the day that Jesus came by. Jesus looked at the man and knew that he had been lying there for a long time. Then Jesus asked the question: "Do you want to be healed?" That would seem to fall into the category of foolish questions. The man had been ill for thirty-eight years. He had been lying in this place in the hope that maybe some day when the waters were troubled he could get into the pool first and be healed. Wasn't it obvious that he wanted to be healed? Why would Jesus ask the man such a question?

But perhaps the answer to the question of Jesus is not so obvious, and perhaps the question is not so foolish as it might appear at first glance. Some reflection suggests that Jesus' question is not irrelevant. Deep down did the man really want to be healed? He said that he wanted to be healed. He had done what he could by going to the pool where he might have a chance of being healed. But was there some reservation within him? Was there at the center some ambivalence about whether he wanted to be healed? After all, he could lie in the shade of the portico while others were working in the hot sun. He didn't have to assume the responsibilities that people who had their health were expected to carry. He had been ill a long time and had established a pattern of life that was familiar and enabled him to survive. To be healed would bring a dramatic change in the way of life for this man. Even though he wanted to be healed, the prospect of making his way as a healthy man in the world must have posed some threat to him. The question of Jesus turns out to be not so foolish after all. Do you want to be healed? Do you genuinely and unreservedly want to be made whole and to experience the profound change in your life which health would bring?

The man didn't respond directly to the question. Rather, he explained why he had not been able to get into the healing waters of the pool. Jesus asked, "Do you want to be healed?" "The sick man answered him, 'Sir, I have no man to put me into the pool when the water is troubled, and while I am going another steps down before me'" (John 5:7). Jesus took that as sufficent evidence that the man did want to be healed. "Jesus said to him, 'Rise, take up your pallet, and walk.' And at once the man was healed, and he took up his pallet and walked" (vs. 8f.).

A notable fact about the healings of Jesus as reported in the four Gospels is that there is no one pattern or process of healing. Sometimes Jesus touches the person to be healed; sometimes he does not. Sometimes Jesus questions the faith of the person to be healed; sometimes he does not. Sometimes, as in the case of the man lying beside the pool, he asks if the person wants to be healed; sometimes he does not. Jesus does not allow a formula to be developed which will guarantee that healing will take place. He does not prescribe a series of steps to be taken in order for healing to occur.

It cannot be said that the desire to be healed must first be established in order for healing to take place. The healing grace of God is not confined by the attitude of any person. Yet the question of Jesus to the man beside the pool is not foolish. The ill do not always want to be healed, and the desire of the person to be made well is a significant factor in the dynamic and complex process of healing. Do you want to be healed? That is a significant question to put to a sick person, a question that needs to be confronted honestly.

In 1964, Norman Cousins became desperately ill with what was diagnosed as a disintegration of the connective tissue in the spine, a condition which was extremely painful. He was given one chance in 500 to recover. The medications he was taking were doing little good. The care he was receiving in the hospital seemed not to be helping. Mr. Cousins reports that he read in a book by Hans Selye, *The Stress of Life*, about the negative effects of negative emotions on body chemistry. Measurable physical changes were caused by emotional tension, frustration, rage, anger. Cousins began to puzzle with the notion that if there were negative effects from negative emotions, could there not be positive effects from positive emotions. He asked himself whether there would be therapeutic value in love and hope and faith and laughter and confidence and the will to live. With the doctors' cooperation, he stopped all the medicines that seemed not to be doing any good and set out on a program of vitamin C injections and affirmative emotions therapy. Included in the affirmative emotions therapy was laughter, which he brought into his life through some films and books. He reports that after an occasion of laughter, he was able to get some sleep and that there was measurable change in the chemistry of the body.

Cousins did not report a quick and easy cure. There was no miracle of complete release from pain. But he did survive. He returned to a productive life. He gave his assessment of his experience in these words: "The will to live is not a theoretical abstraction, but a physiologic reality with therapeutic characteristics."[9]

Do you want to be healed? The answer to the question will

not absolutely open or close the possibilities of healing, but the answer to the question increases or decreases the likelihood of being restored to health. When Jesus sensed that the man by the pool really wanted to be healed, he told him to take up his pallet and walk. And the man "took up his pallet and walked."

The prophet Hosea talked about the illness of his people, about their corruption, wickedness, pride, silliness, greed. He said that they are like a half-baked cake. Furthermore their illness is made all the worse because they do not want to be healed. God lamented about this people: "I would redeem them, but they speak lies against me. They do not cry to me from the heart, but they wail upon their beds; for grain and wine they gash themslves, they rebel against me" (Hos. 7:13f.). God would redeem the people, but they do not ask for God's redemption. There is no healing for the people who do not turn to God or cry to God but wail only for grain and wine. The witness of Hosea is one of many that God longs for people to turn for healing. When they do not, they cut themselves off from what God can do for them, a truth reiterated by Jesus as he asked a man ill for thirty-eight years, "Do you want to be healed?"

"Do you want to be healed?" The question of Jesus is addressed to us. Do we want to be healed of our physical disabilities? Some people don't want to be healed, no matter how often they go to the doctor or how much medicine they take. They enjoy their illnesses and find satisfaction in feeling sorry for themselves because they must suffer such infirmities of the flesh. They like the attention their sickness brings and would miss the demand they make that the doctor listen to them. They use their illness as a way of controlling others and of getting what they want for themselves. Their infirmities enable them to escape from responsibility. They accept all too readily the judgment that their case is hopeless. It is easy to talk about how other people don't want to be healed, but it is not just "they" who find illness satisfying and health threatening. To take seriously the question of Jesus is to probe into our own inner recesses of motivation and desire. "Do you want to be healed?"

Healing of the human body is a mystery. To think positively and to want earnestly to be healed will not necessarily bring instant health. As the healings of Jesus in the Gospels make clear, there is no formula that guarantees healing. There is no act that will invariably heal a wound or reduce a fever or cure a cancer. And the body does not last indefinitely. The death and disintegration of this body we now inhabit is the inevitable end. But there is a grace and power of God in healing. Medicines and surgery and other medical procedures may aid the process. But healing is ultimately a mystery. Jesus healed the physical bodies of people; God continues to minister healing power to people. To want to be healed opens us to the promise and power of God. To want to be healed seems to open channels within us through which the grace of God can flow into our lives. To want to be healed becomes a significant factor in the dynamics of therapy. To want to be healed is to join in trust with the God who wills health and wholeness.

Do you want to be healed? The question is also addressed to us to ask if we want to be healed of the disabilities of the spirit. Jesus Christ offers healing, not only of our bodies but also of our spirits. The question is—Do we want the healing that he offers? Do we want to be healed of our greed? Jesus Christ can help us to be less grasping, to be less dependent on possessions, to be less compulsive about seeking more and more. He can free us from our obsession with possessions. But do we want to be healed? The things we grasp so greedily we find important to us. We don't want to give up our dependence on things. We enjoy our possessions, which we continue to pile up.

As Christ offers to free us from our greed, the question is put to us: "Do you want to be healed?"

Do we want to be healed of our hatred and our desire for vengeance? Jesus Christ can help to free us of these consuming drives. He can enable us to grow in love until we can include in our love even those who have given us reason to hate them. He can offer us such grace of forgiveness that we are able to devote our energy to ways of reconciliation with others rather than to ways of getting even. But do we want to be healed? We find something satisfying about our hatred. There is a perverse enjoyment in trying to find ways to get even with those who wronged us. We delight in contemplating the ways for taking vengeance. Our fantasies are filled with visions of punishment for those who have dared to violate our rights or get in our way.

As Christ offers to free us from our consuming hatreds and our passions for vengeance, the question is put to us: "Do you want to be healed?"

Do we want to be healed of our lusts and our appetites? Jesus Christ can help us deal with the powerful passions. He can help to free us from a lust which compels us to find outlet for our sexual drive in using and abusing other persons, from a lust that drives us to violate relationships we believe most worthy. He can provide us with such a sense of self-worth before God that we have the inner integrity to use our sexual drive rather than to be used by it, to use our appetite for food rather than to abuse it. But we find ourselves ambivalent. We don't like to be driven to violate what we believe to be the good, but we don't want to give up the excitement that is part of the lusting. We want the health that comes with moderation in eating and drinking, but we like the eating and drinking too much to give them up. As Christ offers to free us from the compulsions of our appetites, the question is put to us: "Do you want to be healed?"

Do we want to be healed of our selfishness and our self-centeredness? Jesus Christ can help us to get ourselves a bit out of the center of our universe. He can give us the sensitivity that will enable us to become aware not only of our own needs but of the needs of others. He can enable us to reach out to include others in our universe of concern. Most of all, Jesus puts God at the center of life—his life and our life. In Christ we come to the awareness that the world does not revolve around us, that our wants are not the final determination of what ought to be, that the good is not defined solely from the perspective of what is good for us. But do we want to be healed of the sickness of our selfishness and self-centeredness? We rather like being at the center and believing that the world revolves around us.

A recent book, *Looking Out for #1*, had a powerful appeal because its argument was in line with what most of us want to do anyway. We are ready to devote our lives to looking out for ourselves. Looking out for our interests is not the problem most of us have. The issue is whether life is fulfilled when we have taken care of #1, whether we have been given the gift of life just to get for ourselves. In our Christian conviction we know that life is found by losing it, that life is fulfilled when God and not ourselves is at the center. We know that selfishness and self-centeredness do not fulfill what we are called to be. We know that there is something to life beside putting ourselves at the center, but we like it there. As Christ offers to free us from our self-centeredness, the question is put to us: "Do you want to be healed?"

The question of Jesus to the man sick for thirty-eight years was not a foolish question to him, nor is it to us. "Do you want to be healed?"

14

What Did You Go out to See?

The Question of Jesus
"What did you go out into the wilderness to behold? A reed
shaken by the wind? What then did you go out to see? A man
clothed in soft clothing?" (Luke 7:24-25).

Every summer during my youth, I spent a considerable
amount of time on my grandfather's farm walking behind a mule.
There are not many mules left, but I can report with some
authority that dealing with a mule requires patience and forti-
tude and determination. They were certainly strong animals, but I
was never sure whether they were dumb or obstinate. At any rate,
I could understand the story about the man beating a mule on the
head with a two-by-four. When he was asked what he was doing
to the mule, he replied that he was just trying to get his attention.

Trying to get the attention of people can often be as difficult
as trying to get the attention of a mule. Part of the problem may
be obtuseness, the fact that people are not very responsive to
anything outside themselves. Part of the problem may be that
people are so caught up in what they are doing that it is difficult
to get their attention. Or part of the problem may be that people
have so many claims on their attention that they cease responding
to any of them. One neon sign on a block can be small and quiet,
and still get attention. One neon sign on a block lined with neon
signs may well be lost. In the midst of all the commercials on
television, it takes an authentic genius to design one that gets
attention.

Given such problems, what are the ways of trying to get the attention of people? One can try to hit them over the head with a two-by-four. Perhaps people will hear if the noise is loud enough or will see if the sign is big enough. The decibels on the commercials are turned up, the person selling the breakfast cereal screams the message, each neon sign is bigger and brighter and flashier than the last one. Or one can try to get attention by being clever. Perhaps if the idea is stated in a catchy new way, people will hear it; or if the jingle is cute enough, people will remember it. Or one can try to get attention by coming at people with things that are inherently interesting. Sex and babies and sports figures are used to get people to look. Or one can try to get attention by stressing value. If people sense that something of genuine value is being offered, they will respond.

In many human endeavors people use such ways to get the attention of others. Advertisers are in the business of getting attention and have learned how to hit with a two-by-four. People in politics have to attract attention and get name recognition. People in show business fight vigorously to get their names in big letters. Even religious folk seek ways to get people to pay attention.

Do I have to hit him with a two-by-four? That is the question of the person trying to get the attention of another. But there is another perspective reflected in the question: To what am I going to pay attention? We are trying to get the attention of others, but they are trying to get us to pay attention to them. To ask what we are going to pay attention to raises some significant issues for us. We are not helpless victims who have to respond to the loudest or the cleverest. We can make decisions about what we are going to look at, what we are going to listen to, what we are going to invest energy in, what we are going to pay attention to. None of us can deal with all the information available to us. None of us can respond to all of the appeals made to us. None of us can absorb all the stimuli thrust our way.

What is pushed most blatantly or insistently may break in on us, but we are not passive reactors waiting to respond to the most powerful stimulus. What we pay attention to is partly subject to our control. What we pay attention to says a good deal about us, about the kind of persons we are, about the kind of sensitivities we have, about the kind of interests we have developed. It is a pertinent question to ask: What did you pay attention to? What did you make an effort to comprehend? What are you seeking to find out about? There is a further question to be put to us: Why do we pay attention to what we do? Are we almost entirely at the mercy of the one who yells the loudest, or have we developed some inner direction about what we want to see and hear? Do we determine what is important so that we decide where we invest our limited time and energy, or do we follow the crowd in giving attention to whatever has popular acclaim at the moment?

Jesus once asked a crowd: "What then did you go out to see?" What did you pay attention to, and why did you make the effort to go out to see and hear? John the Baptist had the ability to attract attention. He knew how to generate a crowd. Large crowds come to hear him preach and watch him baptize. John was a colorful character. "Now John wore a garment of camel's hair, and a leather girdle around his waist; and his food was locusts and wild honey" (Matt. 3:4). This strange character suddenly appeared in the wilderness, and by his dress and manner he made people look at him.

John was a vigorous speaker who could break through and make people respond to him. For example, "When he saw many of the Pharisees and Sadducees coming for baptism, he said to them, 'You brood of vipers. Who warned you to flee from the wrath to come?'" (Matt. 3:7). That's provocative language, and the crowd must have loved it when they heard John take out after the "important people" in such an aggressive way. John gained the attention of the people who loved a good scrapper, who delighted in a speaker who minced no words, who cheered the outsider who could take on the establishment.

Some time later John found himself in prison, facing a turn of events which could not have come as a total surprise for one as abrasive and aggressive as John. The crowds were gathered around Jesus now, and he began to talk to them about John, and to press them on why they would pay attention to a man like that. "What did you go out into the wilderness to behold? A reed shaken by the wind?" Of course not. Jesus reminded the people that they were not attracted to John because he happened to be the "in" thing at the moment, because he agreed with anyone who expressed a strong opinion, because he tried to find innocuous ways of saying things so that everyone would agree with him, because he wavered between opposite sides of all issues. They didn't go out to see John because he was a reed shaken by whatever wind happened to be blowing.

Again Jesus asked the question. "Why then did you go out?

To see a man clothed in soft clothing?" Of course not. John was clothed in camel's hair and a leather girdle. They were not attracted to John because he excited them to envy with his luxuries, because he impressed them with his appearance, because he tried to use the religious interests of people to his own gain, because he protected himself against all hardship and offered the same protection to those who would hear and follow him. They didn't go out to see John because he wore fine clothes and made a good thing out of his religion.

Once again Jesus asked the question: "What then did you go out to see? A prophet? Yes, I tell you, and more than a prophet" (Luke 7:26). Jesus pressed the question of why they went to see John and why they paid attention to him. By pressing the question, he reminded them that they had gone out to see John because they had sensed in him an authentic word of God. It wasn't a show that attracted them, although John was a colorful character. It wasn't just the expectation of hearing vigorous talk that attracted them, although John was capable of blasting people and of stating his ideas in memorable terms. Rather they went out to see in the hope of seeing a man authentically manifesting the power of God, and of hearing a word which brought the truth of God into the midst of their common life.

Each of us pays attention to a great many things. The world around us is rich and diverse, and it provides endless possibilities for our exploration. We pay attention to things that relate to the work we do. We pay attention to developments that affect the possibilities of our future. We pay attention to what is happening to the people who mean the most to us. We pay attention to things that happen to interest us. We may know the name of the conductor of every major orchestra in the world and the works that she or he has recorded. We may know the batting average of every player on our favorite baseball team. We may have complete information about every military airplane ever flown. We pay attention to many different things.

For those of us who have come to a faith in God and who have encountered Jesus Christ in our lives, it is needful that we pay attention to the ways of God in our world, that we seek to discern what God is doing in our world, that we listen to hear what God is saying to us. To confront the question of Jesus helps us to focus on what we are looking for. "What did you go out into the wilderness to behold? . . . What then did you go out to see?" Are we looking for a reed shaken by the wind? To look for a reed is to seek someone who will confirm the prejudices and opinions we already hold, who will tells us what they think will please us, who will assure us that God is fully pleased with who we are and what we do. There is an aspect of truth in the popular assertion based on the book titled *I'm OK, You're OK.* But Jesus reminded the crowd that they did not go out to pay attention to John the Baptist because they believed that he would tell them that everything was okay with them and with the world. They went out to see one who trumpeted: "You brood of vipers! Who warned you to flee from the wrath to come? Bear fruit that befits repentance." When we pay attention to the truth of God in our world, we must not only hear from those who tell us that all is okay but from those who bring a high sense of the holiness and goodness and righteousness of God into a world unmistakably corrupt.

"What then did you go out to see?" Are we looking for a man clothed in soft raiment? There are those who will assure us that the highest goal in this life is to be comfortable. There are those who declare that God wants us to be rich in material possessions. There are those who promise that God will reward those who believe in him with worldly success. But Jesus reminded the crowd that they did not go out to see a man who had clothed himself in beautiful garments, a man who had found wealth and ease and comfort as a result of his convictions about the way of God in this world. When we pay attention to the truth of God in our world, we must not hear only from those who talk of the rewards which God offers, but from those who have discerned through Christ that the way of God involves sharing and giving and sacrificing.

"What then did you go out to see?" Are we looking for a prophet? Again Jesus reminded the people that it is indeed a prophet they went out to see in John the Baptist. "What then did you go out to see? A prophet? Yes, I tell you, and more than a prophet. This is he of whom it is written, 'Behold, I send my messenger before thy face, who shall prepare thy way before thee'" (Luke 7:26f.). John came as a prophet to speak the word of God and to bear witness to the one who was coming, even Jesus of Nazareth. Who are we looking for? What are we going out to see? What are we paying attention to? Are we looking for the prophet, for someone who will help us to discern the ways of God, for someone who will speak of the truth of God, for someone who will help us receive Jesus Christ?

We might complain that God is not very good at attracting

attention. Surely if God wanted to do so, God would have no problem in competing with the neon signs and the hard sell. If God had a mind to do so, God could compel our attention. Could not God perform a miracle, or hurl a thunderbolt out of the sky, or speak a word in such a loud voice that we would have to look and listen and believe? But that does not seem to be the way of God with us. God comes into our world, but we have to pay attention. God speaks, but we have to listen. God offers a revelation, but we have to see it and accept it.

Consider the story of Moses and the burning bush. A bush that burns but is not consumed seems a rather spectacular sign, but the biblical account makes clear that Moses had to pay attention. "And Moses said, 'I will turn aside and see this great sight, why the bush is not burnt.' When the Lord saw that he turned aside to see, God called to him out of the bush, 'Moses, Moses!'" (Exod. 3:3f.) When God saw that Moses turned aside to see, then it was that God called to him. Or consider God's manifestation in our world in Jesus Christ. God came in the birth of a child to a woman of an enslaved people in an out-of-the-way corner of the Roman Empire. The child became a man who ruled no lands, conquered no armies, claimed no earthly powers. Nobody had to pay attention to him, and when he was crucified between two thieves on a cross on a hill in Jerusalem, it was hardly big news in the Roman Empire. God doesn't force anyone to pay attention.

What did you go out to see? By his question to them, Jesus reminded the crowd in Jerusalem that when they paid attention to John the Baptist, they were looking for a prophet. By his question to us, Jesus reminds us that if we pay attention, we too can discern the prophet in our midst, the prophet who makes known to us something of God. If we pay attention, we can see the persons who by their devotion and commitment help us to respond to God with greater faithfulness, the persons whose spirits have been nurtured by prayer and meditation so that their lives radiate something of the peace of God, the persons who embody such goodness and love that we see in them an expression of the goodness and love of God, the persons who have a sense of direction about life such that they manifest the purpose of God, the persons who are so sustained and nurtured by the word of the scripture that their lives speak of the word of God.

As we reflect on the things to which we pay attention, the question of Jesus prods us. "What then did you go out to see?" Have we paid attention to those whom God has sent to us to manifest God's will and God's purpose?

15

Was No One Found to Praise God?

The Question of Jesus
"Were not ten cleansed? Where are the nine? Was no one found to return and give praise to God except this foreigner?" (Luke 17:17-18).

Reading Ann Landers can make us aware of significant issues we otherwise might have overlooked, for there are major considerations that all of us miss from time to time. During an extended period, her column generated an astonishing amount of correspondence on the question of whether the toilet paper roll should pull over the top or under the bottom. Many of us had not realized the importance of the question or the many issues involved until Ann Landers provided the opportunity for a full-blown discussion. Her column is testimony to the variety, the range, and the intensity of the problems people have—family problems, money problems, sexual problems, alcohol problems, work problems, school problems, personal discipline problems, body odor problems, and on and on. In reading about the problems people unload on her, we sometimes don't know whether to laugh or to weep.

A woman wrote about a problem she was having with her husband. He didn't beat her, come home drunk, yell at the kids, refuse to change his socks, or cause her any of the usual griefs wives endure. The problem? He wouldn't write a thank-you note, no matter what anyone did for him or gave to him. If Aunt Matilda sent a tie, he wouldn't write a note. If he stayed with friends overnight, he wouldn't write a note. In the total range of human perversity, which regularly is laid out in Ann Landers' column, that may sound like a fairly minor issue. Compared to problems other people have with their spouses, this problem hardly seems critical.

Yet it is cause for concern when a person can't or won't give thanks. Paul took the issue of giving thanks seriously in his letter to the Christians at Rome. At the beginning of the letter he wrote about the wrath of God inflicted upon ungodly and wicked men. He wrote of them: "So they are without excuse; for although they knew God they did not honor him as God or give thanks to him, but they became futile in their thinking and their senseless minds were darkened" (Rom. 1:20f.). Paul used strong language to describe the plight of people who do not honor God or give thanks to God. To fail to give thanks leads to foolishness in the way people think. To fail to give thanks leads to blindness in the way people perceive themselves and their world.

Jesus also expressed concern about people in the condition of being unable or unwilling to give thanks. Ten lepers came to Jesus and pleaded with him to have mercy on them. Lepers were a desperate case, for they suffered from a mutilating disease and were shunned by healthy people who feared they would be contaminated by them. Jesus responded to the plea of the ten lepers for mercy and told them to go and and show themselves to the priests. As they went on their way, they were cleansed of their scourge and healed of their disease. It was a wonderful gift—literally a gift of life for those condemned to a living death. "Then one of them, when he saw that he was healed, turned back, praising God with a loud voice; and he fell on his face at Jesus' feet, giving him thanks. Now he was a Samaritan" (Luke 17:15f.).

Jesus saw the one man who came back and was no doubt pleased with him. But he had a question about the others. "Were not ten cleansed? Where are the nine? Was no one found to return and give praise to God except this foreigner?" Where are the nine? Why doesn't a person write a thank-you note? Why doesn't a person express appreciation when help is given? Where are the nine? We don't know why the nine didn't come back. The scripture doesn't say, and Jesus doesn't speculate about where they are or why they didn't return. But Jesus does seem to think that their failure to return is significant, that it is sign of serious flaw. We can hear the note of incredulity as Jesus asked: "Was no one found to return and give praise to God except this foreigner?" Jesus wasn't peeved because he didn't get the thanks due to him.

100

Jesus' question clearly implies that something was radically wrong with nine lepers who could be healed of a dread disease and not take the trouble to speak a word of praise or thanksgiving to God.

"Was no one found to return and give praise to God except this foreigner?" As we hear this question, we want to say, "Yes, Lord, we're here. We do give you thanks." We are grateful for what God has done for us. But we're not always "here," and the question of Jesus reminds us that we too have taken the gifts of God and gone on our way without praise or thanks. We remember the days when we have not stopped once to give thanks for what God has given to us. We recall the gifts of God we have taken and used without recognition of the Giver. We can understand the behavior of the nine. We have no reason to point the accusing finger at them.

But we do hear the question of Jesus and are prodded by it to want to give thanks. It makes a difference that we want to give thanks, for it motivates us to the effort to learn the language of thanksgiving. It is not easy to say thank you, and the more meaningful or sacrificial the gift, often the more difficult. It is easy to say thank you when someone has opened a door for us, or picked up a paper we have dropped. But how do we express our gratitude to someone who has saved our life, to someone who has sacrificed that we might have an opportunity, to someone who has bailed us out of a frightful difficulty, to someone who has stayed with us day after day in our time of need?

When we turn back to God to give thanks, and when we become part of the grateful Christian community, we can begin to learn the language of thanksgiving. We are helped to say, "Bless the Lord, O my soul; and all that is within me, bless his holy name!" (Psalm 103:1). We are helped to sing, "I give thee thanks, O Lord, with my whole heart; before the gods I sing thy praise" (Psalm 138:1). With practice we learn how to express our gratitude to God, who has given the greatest gifts to all. To be able to express our thanks to God helps as we seek to speak the words of thanks to others who have given much to us.

To hear the question of Jesus, "Was no one found to return and give praise to God except this stranger?" and to want to give thanks is to be made newly aware of the source of all our blessings. "Bless the Lord, O my soul; and forget not all his benefits" (Psalm 103:2). We do many things for ourselves. The necessities of life are not handed to us as we sit passively and wait for the goodies to fall from heaven. Necessities are provided through our efforts. Goals are achieved through our labors. New creations are conceived through our imaginations and brought into being through our skills. We work hard for what we get, and we provide for ourselves through our own labors. There is virtue in being self-sufficient and self-reliant. Among the profound satisfactions of life are those which come when we create and provide through our efforts.

But we miss the fundamental fact of human existence if we think that in any significant sense we are self-sufficient and self-reliant. Ultimately, everything we have is a gift. If we use our talents, they are talents given to us. If we use our energy, it is energy given to us. If we use well the time, it is time given to us. Not one of us created life by our effort. Not one of us willed the sun and the rain and the fertility of the soil. Not one of us set this earth spinning in the vast reaches of the universe. To want to give thanks helps us to new awareness that all we have is a gift. Giving thanks provides a right reading on human existence, and demonstrates that we have come to terms with the reality that we are creatures dependent on the power and grace of God. The words and acts of thanksgiving move us to use all of life as a gift.

To hear the question of Jesus and to want to give thanks enhances the value of the gift and the giver. There are many sources of the value things have for us. An object has value because it is useful. We pay considerable sums of money for cars because cars are useful to us. An object has value because it required the labor of people to produce, and its value bears some relationship to the time and skill required in order to produce it. A thing has value because it is scarce. A person standing by a public water fountain couldn't get much for a glass of water; a person selling a glass of water on a blistering day to people who have no other access to something to drink could command a high price. An object has value when many people want it, and so ticket scalpers can command high prices when mobs of people are trying to get into an event. An object has value when it has an intrinsic worth, which makes people desire it, even though it has little functional use. Gold has remarkably few uses, but gold has attracted people through much of humanity's life on this planet.

But there is another reason that something has value—because of the giver. The drawing a child makes for a parent may have little artistic value and be on a cheap piece of paper, but the drawing has enormous value for the parent when it comes as an expression of the child's love and desire to give. A pin given by a loved one may have little value in a jewelry store, but it may have irreplaceable value for the one to whom it speaks of love offered. An object becomes more precious for us when we know the giver, and when the gift if an expression of love and care. Life becomes more precious for us when we know whose gift it is, when we know that it comes from the God who loves us and cares for us and shares with us. To give thanks to God is an acknowledgment of the gifts given, and to know the giver is to enhance the gift.

To hear the question of Jesus and to want to give thanks restores our health. The woman who wrote to Ann Landers about her husband may not have as critical a problem as the woman whose husband beats her, but she has cause for concern about the condition of her husband. It does strike us that there is something seriously wrong with nine people who could be healed of leprosy and not return to offer a word of gratitude. Paul said of those who did not give thanks that "they became futile in their thinking and their senseless minds were darkened." And what about us? What does our lack of gratitude say about us? If we hear the question of Jesus after the failure of the nine and are moved to our own thanksgiving, we are healthier people. To be able to give thanks expresses the health of our spirits and restores health to our spirits.

Finally, to hear the question of Jesus, "Was no one found to return and give praise to God except this foreigner?" and to want to give thanks helps us to discern the grace and love of God in all that happens to us. There is another word of Paul we should hear, from the Letter to the Ephesians. "And do not get drunk with wine, for that is debauchery; but be filled with the Spirit, addressing one another in psalms and hymns and spiritual songs, singing and making melody to the Lord with all your heart, always and for everything giving thanks in the name of our Lord Jesus Christ to God the Father" (Eph. 5:18-20). Paul makes an extraordinary statement when he says that we give thanks always and for everything. Is that just a bit of Pauline hyperbole? Perhaps. There must be some times when there is no possibility of thanks. There must be some things for which there is no cause for thanksgiving. Yet in every moment of life and in everything that comes to us, we can find the grace and the mercy of God. We would not seek suffering, but in suffering, God has revealed a sustaining presence in our pain. We would not seek sorrow, but sorrow has made us know that nothing can separate us from the love of God. If we seek always and in everything to be thankful, we become aware in fresh ways of what God is constantly doing for us.

We are prodded by the question of Jesus: "Was no one found to return and give praise to God except this foreigner?" When we first meet J.B. and his family in Archibald McLeish's play by that name, they are gathered about the dining room table. With great hilarity they attack the turkey and eat the food of a Thanksgiving dinner. Sarah, J.B.'s wife, enters into the joy of the occasion, and yet she is troubled by what is happening with her family. She wonders if the children and J.B. really know what day it is. J.B. assures her that they do, and when she asks the children what day it is they cry out with laughter: turkey day, cranberry day, stuffing day. But then Sarah breaks in: "Job, I'm serious. Answer your father's question, Jonathan. Tell him what day it is." "Thanksgiving." Sarah presses: "What day is that?" "Thanksgiving Day." And one of the children puts in: "The day we give thanks to God." And another one adds: "For his goodness." Then Sarah asks: "And did you David, Did you Mary? Has any one of you thanked God? Really thanked him? Thanked him for everything?"

Jesus asked: "Was no one found to return and give praise to God except this foreigner?" As we confront that question, we respond with a prayer for the grace that we may live "always and for everything giving thanks in the name of our Lord Jesus Christ to God the Father."

16

Are Grapes Gathered from Thorns?

The Question of Jesus
"Are grapes gathered from thorns, or figs from thistles?" (Matt. 7:16).

At the auction of the estate of Marjorie V. Jackson several years ago, a Cadillac Seville with thirty-seven miles on it was sold. Mrs. Jackson had bought the car new, found that it had a faulty windshield wiper, and had simply abandoned it and bought a new car. There are a number of comments to be made about Mrs. Jackson. She was an eccentric woman. Most people would not abandon a car because of a faulty windshield wiper. They might be annoyed about it, but they would take the car back to have it fixed. She was obviously a rich woman. Not many people can just leave a new Cadillac sitting in the garage and go out to buy a new one. After her death, some five million dollars in cash was found in her house. It must also be said that Mrs. Jackson was a woman of high standards. When a person pays as much for a car as must be paid to get a Cadillac Seville, it is a reasonable expectation that the windshield wipers will work. Mrs. Jackson's new car didn't meet the standard she expected, so she abandoned it and got a new car.

"You get what you pay for." That maxim carries a certain truth, and most of us believe it most of the time. If we buy something cheap, we are not too offended or surprised when it breaks down or falls apart or disintegrates the first time it is used. If we buy something expensive and pay a fair price, we expect to get value for the dollar. If we seek the best and think that we have bought the best, we believe that it should be made of good materials and reflect good workmanship.

In the fallible, imperfect world of human experience, the maxim doesn't always hold true. You get what you pay for—but not always. There are stores in Times Square in New York that are constantly going out of business and advertise great bargains in bold letters. It is doubtful that a customer ever gets a bargain in such places. But there are stores that do have to close and that need to get rid of their goods. The chance of getting a bargain in such a situation is good, and one may actually get more value than was paid for. There are times when people who are selling do not know the value of an antique or a painting, and the buyer gets more value than the money spent.

Sometimes we don't get full value for what we have paid. Expensive but shoddy merchandise is not unknown, and we rightly become indignant when something that ought to work doesn't work. The windshield wipers on a Cadillac Seville ought to work. Most of us cannot afford Mrs. Jackson's indignant response, but we can understand how she felt. Sometimes people don't know the value of what they are buying, and pay far too much for what they receive.

But in general and on the whole we tend to get what we pay for. There are not many astonishing bargains in life, and that seems to be all right. We will always try to beat the system in human affairs and will constantly be looking for the real bargain, of course, but there aren't that many. We will never be too naive in taking an assurance that the price for this particular item is right for the quality received. But there is an assurance in the conviction that, on the whole and in the long run, there are no bargains and that we get what we pay for.

If there is a certain equity and regularity in the realm of human affairs, the realm of the natural world offers an even more persuasive example of the orderliness of our universe. To be sure, even in nature there are aberrations. We thought all the circumstances were right for something to happen, but it didn't. A plant should grow in the environment in which we placed it, but it died. But when we talk about an aberration in nature, we mean that it is an aberration from our perspective. We thought that given the circumstances, we knew what would happen, but we never know the full situation. When something happens that we didn't expect, we set out to find an explanation, always acting in the conviction that nature is orderly. When a plant dies, was it because the soil wasn't right, because it had too much moisture or not enough moisture, because it had too much heat or not enough heat, because it got a bug on it, and on and on.

We don't understand all of the complexities of the world around us, and so we can't make absolute predictions about what will happen. The meteorologists, for example, are certainly not 100 percent accurate in their predictions, but that does not mean that what happens with the weather is haphazard or random. Even with all the sophisticated instruments, meteorologists do not have all the information about what is happening. But the basic assumption about our world is that if they did have complete information, it would be possible to know what results would follow. We operate in a world that we believe to be dependable and orderly. If we put a potato in the ground, we expect with an absolute certainty that we will harvest potatos and not squash. When we plant a cherry tree, we know that we will get cherries and not apples. If the grass doesn't get enough water, there is no doubt that it will turn brown.

There are no bargains in nature where "you get what you pay for." A plant will not yield more than it is able to get from the soil in which it is grown. A fast-growing tree will not provide hard, closely grained wood. Pine lumber will not be like oak lumber. A crop will not survive without adequate moisture.

Jesus knew about the orderliness and dependability of nature when he asked the question, "Are grapes gathered from thorns, or figs from thistles?" In our world the absolute answer to that question is *No*. Thorns and thistles do not produce the fruit we can eat. We don't go to a bush of thorns to gather grapes. We don't go to a thistle bush to gather figs. That's not the way the world works. There are no bargains so that thorns and thistles provide food. But Jesus presses further on the basis of the orderliness of the world. "So, every sound tree bears good fruit, but the bad tree bears evil fruit. A sound tree cannot bear evil fruit, nor can a bad tree bear good fruit" (Matt. 7:17-18). It is not just that there is no fruit to be gotten from trees that don't bear fruit but also that the quality of the fruit is dependent on the quality of the tree. A bad tree will not bear good fruit. There are no bargains. It takes a good tree to bring forth good fruit.

If there are no bargains in the long run in human affairs, if there are no bargains in nature where we have to deal with the hard facts of the world as it is, it is also true that there are no bargains in the life of the Spirit. Jesus talked about the false prophets who put up a good outward appearance. "Beware of false prophets, who come to you in sheep's clothing but inwardly are ravenous wolves" (Matt. 7:15). In the realm of religion as in every other area of human experience, there are those who will deceive others, those who will use the needs of others to their own enrichment, those who will play upon the hopes and fears of others to take advantage of them. Religion has no monopoly on charlatans in our world, but religion has its fair share of false prophets. One example will suffice. An "evangelist" sent a letter filled with pious talk about the power of prayer and what his prayers could do for the recipient. Enclosed with the letter was a piece of cloth, which the evangelist asked to be returned to him so that it could be prayed over and then sent back. Also enclosed with the letter was a contribution card with the clear message that if the piece of cloth was going to be effective in healing, some money had better be sent. It was implied, furthermore, that the more money sent, the better the healing power of the piece of cloth. Jesus had the word for such people. "Beware of false prophets, who come to you in sheep's clothing but inwardly are ravenous wolves."

Not all the false prophets are as blatant or crude as the evangelist hawking his prayer cloths. Among all the varieties of religious claims, how is one to tell what is true? The religious page of any city newspaper gives impressive testimony to the number and variety of people who offer their way in the religious life, and who invite all to come and share the truth they have found. How are such people to be judged? How are claims to be tested? Again, Jesus offers the word for making the judgment and testing the claims. "You will know them by their fruits. Are grapes gathered from thorns, or figs from thistles?"

The warning of Jesus that there are no bargains in the life of the Spirit is helpful as we seek to discern the truthfulness and integrity of those who would tell us of God and invite us to follow the ways of God. There is a way to test whether people speak the truth, whether they speak out of honest commitment. The question of Jesus, "Are grapes gathered from thorns, or figs from thistles?" is addressed to people whom he is trying to help deal with the false prophets who would deceive them and manipulate them.

But the question of Jesus has another thrust. The certainty of Jesus that there are no bargains in the life of the Spirit takes on different significance as we ponder our own lives. The bad tree cannot bear good fruit; therefore, the quality of our lives determines the kind of fruit we will be able to bear. Most of us are caught in a certain amount of deception as we try to impress others with who we are. We would like for others to think we are better than we are. We cherish a good reputation, and are pleased when people speak well of us. And sometimes we try to substitute that surface impression for genuine goodness. We become adept at doing things that receive favorable public notice, and manage to insure that the good we do does not go unnoticed. There are times when we seek to deceive ourselves. We don't want to confront in any depth who we are, and so we hide from ourselves. We want to be good, or virtuous, or fruitful, but we don't want to pay the price to become the kind of person who can produce goodness, or virtue, or the fruits of the Spirit. The question of Jesus forces a new assessment. "Are grapes gathered from thorns, or figs from thistles?" The assertion of Jesus brings a measure of realism. "So, every sound tree bears good fruit, but the bad tree bears evil fruit. A sound tree cannot bear evil fruit, nor can a bad tree bear good fruit." There are no bargains in the life of the Spirit.

Jesus uses the image of the good tree and the fruit which it bears. The Apostle Paul puts some content into that image, when he writes to the Galatians about the fruit of the Spirit, the fruit that is borne by one in whom the Spirit dwells. "The fruit of the Spirit is love, joy, peace, patience, kindness, goodness, faithfulness, gentleness, self-control" (Gal. 5:22f.). Paul's words can lead us to look at our situation in two ways. On the one hand, he helps us to see what we would look for in human experience and relationships when we want to find out if people are bearing good fruit. Are they showing love in the way they deal with one another? Do they communicate a profound sense of the joy of life? Do they radiate an inner peace, and do they seek to live at peace with others, and are they effective in enabling people to live at peace with one another? Are they quick-tempered and short-fused with others, or can they bear the shortcomings and provocations of others with patience? By his description of the fruits of the Spirit, Paul points us to specific situations and actions.

On the other hand, Paul's words help us to see what kind of people we need to be if we are to be the good tree, which bears good fruit. It's tough business trying to love when we are not a loving person. It's tough business to try to express joy in our world when we have no joy within us. It's tough business to bring peace into our world when our own spirits are torn with strife. It's tough business trying to be patient when we are harried and tense. Or, if Jesus is right, it's more than just tough to bear the fruit of the spirit if our inner life is all wrong; it's impossible. "Are grapes gathered from thorns, or figs from thistles?" If within ourselves we are empty and corrupt and angry and selfish, we simply do not produce love and joy and peace and patience.

We need to take thought about how we can best demonstrate the love we have, for it is not always clear what the loving expression is. With all of the things Paul describes as the fruit of the Spirit, there is need for thought about how we can bring them effectively into our relationships with others. Love may require us to chastise another. Patience does not mean unending acceptance of whatever another happens to want to do. But the first concern is not with how we can show love and joy and peace and patience. The first concern is whether we are the kind of person who can bear such fruit at all. The first concern is not with what we do but with what we are. The first concern is not with the kind of fruit we are bearing but with the kind of tree we are.

Again a word from Paul can help us fill out what it means to talk about becoming the kind of person who can bear good fruit. Paul writes to the Colossians that he has heard about their love in the Spirit, and then says: "And so, from the day we heard of it, we have not ceased to pray for you, asking that you may be filled with the knowledge of his will in all spiritual wisdom and understanding, to lead a life worthy of the Lord, fully pleasing to him, bearing fruit in every good work and increasing in the knowledge of God" (Col. 1:9f.). If we are to manifest the fruit of the Christian life, we need to become the kind of people who can express something of the spirit of Jesus Christ in what we say and do. The prayer of Paul for the Colossians is appropriate for us as we seek to become such persons, filled with a knowledge of the will of God, having spiritual wisdom and understanding.

That kind of life is nurtured through prayer, through listening to the word of God, through meditation and reflection, through joining with the Christian community in the worship of God, through conscious effort to nurture the good within us, through openness to the presence of Christ. There is no formula that will bring us health. There is no one set of exercises that will bring us health. As each person must find his or her own way to physical health, each of us must find our own way to spiritual health. But though there are no formulas that guarantee physical health, there are guidelines: good food, adequate exercise, sufficient rest. And there are guidelines for spiritual health. It is not a matter of so many minutes of prayer every day, but it is a matter of relating to God in prayer. It is not a matter of so many Bible verses a day, but it is a matter of listening to what God is revealing to us through the scripture. It is not a matter of this pattern of meditation and reflection, but it is a matter of finding the time to let ourselves think about who we are and where we are going and what God has done for us.

The questions of Jesus points to the hard reality of our life: "Are grapes gathered from thorns, or figs from thistles?" There are no bargains in the life of the Spirit. We are either the kind of person who can manifest the fruit of the Spirit or we are not. So the prayer of Paul for his people becomes our prayer for ourselves, the prayer that we "may be filled with the knowledge of his will in all spiritual wisdom and understanding, to lead a life worthy of the Lord."

17

Why Do You Not Know How to Interpret?

The Question of Jesus
"You know how to interpret the appearance of earth and sky; but why do you not know how to interpret the present time?" (Luke 12:56).

The contemporary world is proud of its sophistication, but it's not entirely clear that there has been a great deal of progress from earlier times in interpreting the present and forecasting the future. Take weather forecasting for example. There is a whole discipline of metereology, and weather forecasters have all those charts with lines showing barometer readings from all over the world, computers, wind flow indicators, satellite pictures, and what have you. But they still can't give an absolutely firm word about what the weather will be tomorrow, and they manage to miss tomorrow's weather entirely on more than a few occasions. Scientific forecasters do better than *The Farmer's Almanac*, but then they don't take the long view as the *Almanac* does. The picture of someone sitting in an office somewhere predicting what the weather is going to be in every section of the country fifteen months ahead is a bit mind boggling.

Weather forecasting with all of its uncertainties is brought to mind by the example Jesus used. "He also said to the multitudes, 'When you see a cloud rising in the west, you say at once, "A shower is coming"; and so it happens. And when you see the south wind blowing, you say, "There will be scorching heat"; and it happens'" (Luke 12:54f.). Jesus pointed to people who could read the signs and apparently with considerable success could forecast what the weather would be on the morrow. It's not clear that today's forecasters with all their sophisticated information do any better than the people who could interpret the cloud from the west and the wind from the south.

Not only in weather forecasting but in many other areas of life, people try to read the signs in the present to discern what is happening and what is going to happen. Economists spend a lot of time with endless statistics in the effort to tell us which way the economy is moving. During the political season, the pollsters take their scientifically balanced samples in the effort to tell who is going to win the election. The odds-makers do intensive studies of the combatants on the sports' fields in the effort to tell who is going to win the World Series or the Superbowl.

To be successful at forecasting takes both information and skill. The weather forecaster has to know what the barometric pressures are; the economist has to have the figures on the gross national product and retail sales; the pollster needs to get the information about what groups of voters say they are going to do. Without the information there is no way of knowing what is happening or of predicting what will happen. But forecasting also takes sensitivity and skill and insight. Sheer facts don't reveal very much. It takes an interpreter who knows what the facts mean to figure out what is happening and what is coming. A barometric pressure reading by itself means nothing until it is set in the context of other readings and until the forecaster figures out what those readings mean.

Such intense efforts are made in trying to understand weather and economic developments and political elections because it is important to us to discern what is happening now and what the prospects are for the future. If we can't read the signs, we lack the ability to interpret what is going on. We may deal with things as they happen, but we have no sense of what the broader movements of events are. We need to try to discern the shape of the future so that we can take the actions in the present to prepare for what is coming. Forecasting in any area is not an exact science. But even if the future is not foretold with total accuracy, it is important to make the effort to discern the signs of where we are and where we are going.

Jesus wondered about the people of his time who failed to discern the signs of what was happening to them. "When you see

113

a cloud rising in the west, you say at once, 'A shower is coming'; and so it happens. And when you see the south wind blowing, you say, 'There will be scorching heat'; and it happens. You hypocrites! You know how to interpret the appearance of earth and sky; but why do you not know how to interpret the present time?"

What is Jesus talking about when he speaks of interpreting the present time? He isn't talking about what the market is going to be for clay pots, or who is going to be the next Roman governor, or what the odds are for the big chariot race. He is talking about discerning what is happening to the soul or the spirit of the people, about perceiving what the possibilities are for this people to be faithful to God. Jesus himself is a sign, and the issue for his people is whether they can discern what his coming means. Can they see what God is doing in their midst, and can they respond to what is happening so that they may continue to be God's people in the coming days? Jesus said that sadly the people do not know how to interpret the present time, so that they are missing what is happening and threatening their hopes for the future.

There is an urgency about Jesus' question, "Why do you not know how to interpret the present time?" They are missing the meaning of who they are and what they are doing. They are oblivious to the important things for their future that are taking place. They can't do the things that need to be done today to make ready for what is coming. One way to understand the faithfulness of the saints extolled in the Book of Hebrews is to see them as people who could discern the signs of their times and then could act on what they saw. Because they could discern and act, significant things happened for them and their people. "By faith Noah, being warned by God concerning events as yet unseen, took heed and constructed an ark for the saving of his household" (Heb. 11:7). Somehow Noah discerned the threat that was coming and made ready to meet it. "By faith Abraham obeyed when he was called to go out to a place which he was to receive as an inheritance; and he went out, not knowing where he was to go" (Heb. 11:8). Somehow Abraham discerned the need to move, and he went.

Why did the people to whom Jesus talked, and why do we, not know how to interpret the present time? Why can they and we read the signs of the weather but miss what is going on at the heart of our life? It is possible to speculate about many reasons.

People are indifferent or preoccupied with many other things. People lack the sensitivity to discern the signs of the times, or they willfully blind themselves to what is happening because they fear to know. People fail to develop the capacity to understand and interpret the signs.

Jesus' question confronts us: "Why do you not know how to interpret the present time?" There are signs that need to be interpreted so that we can understand what is happening to us and where we are moving. There is the increasing willingness in our society to depend on gambling, to exploit the weakness and greed of people, in order to pay for the cost of government. There is the deep and eager yearning for the nurture of the life of the spirit. There is the increasing number of stores and business places open on Sunday. There is the willingness of our nation to push and profit from the sale of military armaments. There is the sustained and serious quest for a meaning in life beyond the external marks of success. There is the willingness to provide money for armaments partly on the basis that it helps employment, and the hesitation to provide money for jobs in arts or health or housing. There is the urgent concern about food for the world. There is the increasing awareness of the impact of what we do on our environment.

The future is no clearer for us than it was for Noah, or for Abraham, who went out not knowing where he was to go. We get mixed signals about where we are, and what's happening to us, and where we are going. But the question of Jesus pushes us to the urgent importance of seeking to understand where we are, and what God's will for us is in this time. "Why do you not know how to interpret the present time?"

18

Is Not Life More than Food?

The Question of Jesus
"Is not life more than food, and the body more than clothing?"
(Matt. 6:25).

Some people have trouble getting cakes or pies cut into pieces of equal size. A pie is carefully cut in half, and the valiant effort is made to cut the half into thirds. But somehow the first third of the half turns out to be bigger than the third third of the half. There is a surefire, absolutely accurate way to get a piece of cake cut in half, however. It is to offer to divide the cake between two children and to let one of the children cut it and let the other child get the first choice of which piece to take. Children can get in to vicious squabbles over who gets the most food, or who gets to lick the bowl of chocolate cake batter, or who ate all the pudding that was left in the refrigerator.

It is not only children who get caught up in passions about food. Paul seems to have found some problems about food in the church at Corinth. "When you meet together, it is not the Lord's supper that you eat. For in eating, each one goes ahead with his own meal, and one is hungry and another is drunk. . . . Do you despise the church of God and humiliate those who have nothing? What shall I say to you?" (1 Cor. 11:21f.). Paul was dismayed at the way the people in the church were behaving when it came to eating. They gobbled up their food, apparently so that those who had enough wouldn't have to share with those who were hungry. The picture of people sitting around a church dinner stuffing themselves, while other people sat around without anything to eat, is not exactly an edifying one, and we can share in Paul's dismay.

We spend a lot of time on food.

Planning food. Experts advise making a list before venturing to the store to guard against the enticements of those who know how to place their wares so we will encounter them in a weakened condition and succumb to the compulsion to respond to hunger pangs by grabbing everything we see. And there is concern about a balanced diet, getting the right combination of tastes for a meal, and fixing a plate with colors that go well together.

Buying food. Some people grow food for themselves or for others, but most of us have to make regular trips to the supermarket, a process that can turn out to be time consuming. There are many decisions to make in choosing among the brands and can sizes and packing styles. It all leads to the trauma of the checkout counter, when the cash register runs up what seems close to the national debt.

Preparing food. Even frozen foods have to be put in the oven, and there are many still dedicated to the notion that there is some culinary goodness to be found in boiling and baking and broiling and stewing for oneself.

Eating food. We spend time not only in the physical act of eating but in anticipating the food that is coming. We spend other time in regret after the meal is over, usually regretting that we have eaten so much.

Cleaning up after food. There are the inevitable dishes and pots and pans that have to be cared for, and leftovers which have to be disposed of.

Snacking on food. Between meals there are the coffee breaks and tea breaks and happy hours and TV snacks and before-bed raids on the refrigerator.

All in all we spend a lot of time and energy dealing with food.

In the midst of all this activity relating to what we eat, a question of Jesus raises an issue of some significance. "Is not life more than food?" Because we spend so much time with food, because food is absolutely essential to our survival, because eating food can be such a satisfying experience, we may find that the events of food become the dominant events of life. There are people for whom the high points of every day are the meals. So the question of Jesus speaks to the situation of many of us when he asks if life isn't more than food. He is not just asking whether there isn't more to life than relishing good food. He is asking whether there isn't more to life than physical survival, whether there isn't more to life than sustaining our bodies, whether there isn't more to life than satisfying our appetites.

The answer to the question for Jesus is clear and unambiguous. Is not life more than food? *Yes.* There is more to life than relishing good food. There is also more to life than sheer physical survival, more to life than sustaining our bodies, more to life than satisfying our appetites. Jesus never denied the importance of food, and his feeding a multitude of people on more than one occasion is evidence that he certainly knew that people had to eat. In the prayer he taught his disciples, he led them to pray for their daily bread. There are a number of references in the Gospels to occasions when Jesus shared meals with people, and his enemies were not above charging that he ate and drank too much. But Jesus is clear that eating is not the supreme end of life, that eating is not the sum and substance of life, that eating is not the greatest good in life. The devil tempted Jesus to make bread the center of his ministry as he invited Jesus to turn stones into bread. But Jesus met the devil's invitation with the unequivocal response: "Man shall not live by bread alone" (Matt. 4:4).

"Is not life more than food?" To give an unequivocal answer to that question can do a number of things for us. First, if we know that life is more than food, we are freed from anxious concern about food and about our physical existence. Jesus spoke these words of comfort and assurance to his followers even as he confronted them with the question about the meaning of food. "Therefore I tell you, do not be anxious about your life, what you shall eat or what you shall drink, nor about your body, what you shall put on. Is not life more than food, and the body more than clothing?" (Matt. 6:25). We have to take thought in order to provide the food we need to survive. The labors of many people make possible the food on our table—the farmer, the processor, the transporter, the wholesaler, the retailer. We do not survive on manna that falls from heaven. Jesus does not deny that we have to work for the food we eat. His word is that we do not have to be anxious about our lives, about what we eat or drink. Our existence is not defined by the food we eat. The question of Jesus helps us to remember that life is more than food and the body is more than clothing. Because God makes provision for all of life, we do not have to be anxious about the lesser things.

118

Second, if we know that life is more than food, we will be enabled to use food properly. Food is important. The preparation of food takes time and energy. Eating food is properly more than just consuming the energy needed to keep our bodies alive, for eating food can be a significant social occasion that has impact on human relationships. There is something that feels right to us when we eat together on important occasions. There is a sense of shared community among people who have eaten together. The people who gather together around the same table on festival occasions have created new bonds or have strengthened the bonds which already existed between them. The person who takes the time to prepare good food for others expresses care and concern for those who will eat the food.

Because food is so important in so many ways, it is easy to get a distorted perspective on just how important it is. For some, food becomes the most important fact of life. Their days focus on the food they eat. The high moments of each day are the times of eating. Food becomes a solace and a comfort. As each new day is anticipated, the occasions of eating make the day bearable. Survival is a matter of getting from breakfast to coffee break, from coffee break to lunch, from lunch to snack, from snack to dinner, and from dinner to goodies consumed before the TV. But life is more than food, and to know that is to gain an appropriate understanding of the role that food plays within the larger perspective of human existence.

One person grew in her awareness of the role of food in life through fasting. Cathy Dunn wrote of her experience: "I fasted one day a week for a year, and one of the things fasting did was to give me a much clearer awareness of my relationship to food—of why I eat for example. Often it's not simply to satisfy my hunger but because I'm bored or feel I'm owed some pleasure. . . . Fasting makes me feel lighter, cleaner. It creates an easiness in living and helps my meditation." Fasting may be one way to get clear that life is more than food and to get clear on a proper way of dealing with food. But there are other ways to find the "more" of life and to use food not as an end but as a means to enable us to find the enrichment of our lives.

Third, if we know that life is more than food, we will be enabled to share our food. Concern about the food we have to eat is legitimate, but concern about the food we have to eat becomes corrupt when we fail to remember that life is more than food. Concern for the food for others is a theological concern, one way in which we are faithful and responsive to God. When we are freed from compelling passions about food, we are able to be concerned about the hunger of others. Part of the "more" of life is to use the resources that have been granted to us not solely for the satisfaction of our appetites and needs but to meet the hunger and needs of others.

When we know that life is more than food, we are not satisfied with feeding our physical bodies; we are not compelled to spend inordinate resources in securing the finest and fanciest of foods; we are not limited in our satisfactions to those given by what we taste. A whole new world of joy and satisfaction and fulfillment is opened to us as we can be concerned not only with feeding ourselves but with providing food for others.

Finally, if we know that life is more than food, we can be blessed in abundant ways by the food we do eat. As we take in food well and wisely, our physical bodies are blessed with health and strength. But as we truly eat well and wisely, our lives are blessed as the food we eat becomes the expression of God's concern for us. People must labor for the food they eat—the soil must be cultivated, the seeds must be planted, the crop must be harvested, the food must be processed, and on and on. Most of us earn the food we eat. But none of us provides the energy of the sun or the fertility of the earth. Food, which sustains our lives, is God's gift.

Christians gather regularly at the Lord's Table to celebrate the Eucharist, to remember the last supper Jesus shared with his disciples, to enter anew into communion with their Lord. On that table is bread and wine, and the gathered people eat and drink. In some small way, presumably the physical body is nurtured by what is eaten at that table. But that food nurtures the whole person, that food is affirmation of God's love and care for us in the life and death and resurrection of Jesus Christ. When we know that life is more than food, then God can minister through this bread to bless all of life.

The question of Jesus helps us to gain perspective not only on the food we eat but on the whole of our existence. "Is not life more than food?"

19

Why Do You Transgress?

The Question of Jesus
"And why do you transgress the commandment of God for the sake of your tradition?" (Matt. 15:3).

There are some classic scenes of parent-child relationships, scenes that somehow capture the essence of a particular phase in the dynamic interaction between a parent and a child. Norman Rockwell painted one such classic scene when he showed a mother with a smile of infinite bliss on her face holding a cup of coffee, and through the window the child can be seen getting on the bus for the first day of school in the fall. There are many other scenes that can be visualized—parents holding the newborn baby, parents comforting the child who has fallen on roller skates, parents cheering for the little leaguer, parents watching as the child walks across the stage to receive a diploma.

There is one other scene that has taken place in the relationship of almost every parent and child. The parent with angry face stands over the child with abject countenance to demand an answer to the question: Why did you do that? The "that" can be almost anything. Why did you throw the ball through the window of the neighbor's garage? Why did you take the scarf from the store when you had money in your purse to pay for it? Why did you sneak a smoke in a forbidden area at the school? Why did you stay out two hours later than the deadline?

Parents often press hard in their demand for the child to give some reason for doing wrong. Such pressure is an expression of the parents' frustration and anger. They know there isn't any good reason why the child did a bad thing, and deep down they are aware there isn't much the child can say. Nonetheless they keep demanding that the child give some explanation for what was done. Sometimes, to be sure, the reason why the child went astray is clear, at least to the parent, and the parent believes that the child will be helped by facing squarely why the wrong was done. If the child articulates that the wrong was done because of pressure from peers, or because of carelessness, or because of greed, then perhaps the child will learn from the experience. Sometimes the reason why the child went astray is not obvious, but the parent senses that something not clearly recognized is at work. Perhaps the child's actions are saying something about herself, or perhaps the child is expressing some problem in the relationship with the parents. Pressure to articulate the reason for the wrong behavior may help to uncover some of the hidden dynamics at work.

Unless the demand is entirely the venting of anger and frustration by the parent, it is important for encounter to take place between the parent and child. It is important for both the parent and the child to try to understand why something happened. People are able to deal with situations more adequately when they understand what is going on. There is a possibility for change if people figure out what is driving them in directions they don't want to go. Understanding of why they behave as they do can show people where they are most vulnerable and help them to be on their guard. Motivations are frequently complex, but when there is some glimmer about the inner dynamic, people are less at the mercy of the driving forces within themselves.

The Pharisees and the scribes confronted Jesus and wanted to know why his disciples didn't wash their hands before they ate; they wanted to know why the disciples were transgressing. Several things seem to lie behind that question. The Pharisees and the scribes used the question as a way of calling attention to a practice of which they disapproved. They were offended when they saw people who were claiming a special religious commitment ignoring one of the practices that served as a sign of real religious interest. One of the ways to point out what they saw was to press Jesus with the question about why the disciples transgressed in this matter. To ask the question was also their way of raising the question of whether Jesus respected their traditions or whether he was putting himself above all that. In effect they were saying: Jesus, why don't you make your disciples wash their hands? Don't you think our traditions are important?

Then to ask the question was also to try to establish the authority of the tradition. They must have hoped to get Jesus into a position where he would have to acknowledge the legitimacy of the practice. Most people did not follow all the ritual practices; the ordinary person didn't have time for all of that. But probably most people believed that it was important for the religious leaders to wash their hands before they ate and to do all the other things the tradition required. By their question about why the disciples transgressed, the Pharisees were putting Jesus in a position where he had to take a stand on the validity of the tradition. If he said that the tradition had authority, then they could press the issue of why the disciples didn't obey it. If he said that the tradition had no authority, then he would offend many people. The Pharisees and the scribes had some point to make by pressing the question on Jesus as to why his disciples transgressed.

The second time in the passage in Matthew that the question is asked, it is put by Jesus. Jesus didn't answer directly the question the Pharisees asked about why the disciples transgressed. He didn't say such rituals were unimportant. He didn't say that the disciples had too much other important work to do to spend time on such matters. He didn't say that the disciples were careless slobs and that he would see that they shaped up. Rather, Jesus responded to the question about his disciples' transgression with a question of his own. "He answered them, 'And why do you transgress the commandment of God for the sake of your tradition?'" (Matt. 15:3). They had asked Jesus why his disciples transgressed the tradition of the elders. Jesus shot back the far more serious question about why they themselves transgressed the commandment of God.

Was this question of Jesus just an effective way of turning aside the question the Pharisees put to him, or did he have some basis for the charge that they transgressed the commandment of God? Jesus was specific about the way in which the Pharisees put their tradition above the requirement of the command of God. "For God commanded, 'Honor your father and your mother,' and, 'He who speaks evil of father or mother, let him surely die.' But you say, 'If any one tells his father or his mother, What you would have gained from me is given to God, he need not honor his father.' So, for the sake of your tradition, you have made void the law of God. You hypocrites!" (Matt. 15:4-7). Apparently in their teaching, the Pharisees said that a pledge to give to God had to be honored, even if what had been promised to God was needed to care for a father or mother. Jesus charged them with hypocrisy in their interpretation of honoring the tradition, for the religious establishment of which the Pharisees were part was supported by the gifts people pledged to give to God.

"Why do you transgress the commandment of God for the sake of your tradition?" By his question, Jesus pressed the issue of their priorities. It is important to insist that the commitments that people make be honored. If they promise to give something to God, it is not a pledge to be taken lightly. But commitments and responsibilities are not assumed and fulfilled in isolation. One commitment must be weighed against other obligations, and decisions must be made about what has the greatest claim. As the question of Jesus makes clear, the priorities of the Pharisees had gotten badly skewed when they put greater claim on the tradition of keeping a pledge to God than they put on the commandment of God to care for father and mother. The question of Jesus raised the issue of what kind of claim God had on their lives and how that claim of God was experienced. The question of Jesus forced a consideration of what their actions meant when seen in the context of their broader relationship to God and God's commandments.

Why do you transgress? If someone asks us why we did a wrong, we find that a searching and difficult question to deal with. "Why do you transgress the commandment of God?" We find that question of Jesus even more searching and difficult. But surely it is important that we hear Jesus asking that question of us as well as of the Pharisees. When we face that question, we are pressed to recognize the seriousness of our failures, for it is the commandment of God that we transgress. The question of Jesus forces us to look again at what we are doing and what our actions mean. The question of Jesus reminds us that there is an accountability for what we do with our lives, that we have to answer for the way in which we make our decisions and deal with others. To face the question of Jesus helps us to deal with ourselves as we not only look at what we do but probe why we do it.

"Why do you transgress the commandment of God?" As we ponder that question, we may have to acknowledge that what Jesus said about the Pharisees is true about us. "For the sake of your tradition, you have made void the law of God" (v. 6). It may be religious tradition that gets in the way of our responding to the

124

call of God. We get so focused on a point of doctrine, or a way of organizing the church, or a style of worship, that we shatter the body of Christ and even violate the commandment of God to love one another. Points of doctrine and ways of organizing and styles of worship are meaningful and important, but when they lead to bickering and animosity and separation and strife, the question of Jesus presses with particular urgency: "Why do you transgress the commandment of God for the sake of your tradition?"

Or it may be other traditions that stand against our obedience to the commandments of God. We have become comfortable with a certain way of organizing life and carrying on our activities. Even though our ways issue in injustice for many, we are reluctant to seek justice if it means too much change. We don't want to be so wasteful of the scarce resources of our earth, but how do we get out of the consumption patterns to which we have become accustomed? We don't want to hurt anyone, but if what is demanded for us to get ahead requires it, we have to do what everybody else does. "Why do you transgress the commandment of God?" Because, Lord, it's so hard to be different when God's commandments move against our traditional ways.

Then there are times when we have to respond to Jesus' question by confessing that we didn't know we were transgressing the commandment of God. A number of years ago, Rachel Carson wrote the book that began to raise a general awareness about what we were doing to our planet, which God entrusted to our care. Sometime later Michael Harrington wrote about the invisible poor and brought into fresh consciousness the blighted lives of the people who barely exist in the midst of our affluence. The Black Power movement was in part an effort to raise the consciousness of black and white alike to what was being done to people who were looked at as inferior and who thought of themselves as inferior. Liberation theologians speak in firm voice about the injustice done to minority and oppressed people around the world, especially in Third World countries. We have become at least a bit more sensitive to the ways in which our society has failed to deal with the difficulties of the handicapped. The hurt inflicted on the gay community has been brought to public awareness, hurt inflicted by those who not only have strong convictions about homosexuality but manifest their convictions in hatred for the gay person.

When issues have been focused for us in new ways, we look

back and wonder how we could have been so blind, how we could have been so insensitive, how we could have inflicted such hurt on other people, how we could have transgressed the commandments of God so flagrantly. All we can say in answer to the question of Jesus is that we did not know what we were doing. The question causes us to ponder what we are doing today that will be seen, in the light of future understandings, to be hurtful and destructive of our world, of others, and of ourselves. "Why do you transgress the commandment of God?" Because, Lord, we don't use our eyes and ears and minds and imaginations and hearts to know what we are doing.

Finally, there are times when we have to respond to Jesus' question by confessing that there isn't any good reason why we hurt others and ourselves, why we do the evil instead of the good. Somehow we just do it. We seem to be in the grip of compulsions beyond our control. We don't want to speak the spiteful word of gossip, but we do it. We don't want to be so picky and selfish, but we can't seem to help it. We don't want to eat too much and drink too much, but we do. Paul shared our condition and described it when he wrote: "I do not understand my own actions. For I do not do what I want, but I do the very thing I hate. . . . For I do not do the good I want, but the evil I do not want is what I do. Now if I do what I do not want, it is no longer I that do it, but sin which dwells within me" (Rom. 7:15, 19f.). "Why do you transgress the commandment of God?" Lord, because we sometimes just can't help ourselves. There is indeed sin within us.

We confront our children with their mistakes not to condemn them but to help them. The question of Jesus confronts us not to condemn us but to help us. To discern the pressures upon us, to become aware of our blindness, to know why we are often in the grip of compulsions within us can free us to accept the grace and power of God, which strengthens us for love and obedience.

20

Why Did You Doubt?

The Question of Jesus
"O man of little faith, why did you doubt?" (Matt. 14:31).

There is a children's card game called I Doubt It. In the game, players may claim to have cards they do not actually have. When a player does claim to have a card, the other players have to decide whether they believe the card is really held. If a player decides to challenge another, the player calls out "I doubt it."

It is important to develop a certain skepticism about all we read and hear. We need to learn to say "I doubt it." An appropriate response to the inflated advertising which claims that a routine movie is the most thrilling show ever made is an "I doubt it." When politicians finish the recital of all that will be accomplished if only they are elected to office, a realistic response is "I doubt it." When the encyclopedia salesperson finishes the pitch about how life will be enriched and transformed by the purchase of this set, an honest assessment of human possibilities leads one to murmur "I doubt it." When the preacher gets too vehement in sweeping proclamations of absolute truth, it's a healthy check to murmur to oneself "I doubt it."

Particularly in the realm of religion it is important to keep a measure of skepticism, for in the name of religion, people are sometimes given to making inflated claims. Speaking on behalf of God, people have promised a guaranteed way to find health, happiness, and prosperity. Religion can be offered as the solution to all the problems that plague the human species. It's a mark of healthy realism to meet such extravagant claims with a skeptical "I doubt it."

Religious types often seem tempted to make dogmatic assertions about things that are beyond the realm of human certainty. People can claim to know too much about God and about the ways of God. People can be too positive about what God wants other people to do. People can assert what is the will of God when they cannot possibly know the will of God. A man who had deserted his family, married a girl half his age, and joined a commune wrote back to a friend stating that God had told him that his friend should come and join him. The friend wrote back that he found the directive from God very interesting and that when God told him directly that he should do it, he would. The assertion that God wants you to do something is well met with a questioning "I doubt it."

How do we deal with the incident described by Matthew when the disciples got into a boat to go across the sea to Gennesaret and Jesus remained behind to pray? "When evening came, he was there alone, but the boat by this time was out on the sea, beaten by the waves; for the wind was against them. And in the fourth watch of the night he came to them, walking on the sea. But when the disciples saw him walking on the sea, they were terrified, saying, 'It is a ghost!' And they cried out for fear. But immediately he spoke to them, saying, 'Take heart, it is I; have no fear.' And Peter answered him, 'Lord, if it is you, bid me come to you on the water.' He said, 'Come.' So Peter got out of the boat and walked on the water and came to Jesus . . ." (Matt. 14:23-29). What's our response to all that? Are we willing to accept that story, or are we likely to say "I doubt it."

Before we decide about this story of Jesus and Peter walking on the water, it is important to note that while we need to develop a measure of skepticism, it is possible to push doubt too far. Why do we doubt? What leads us to say "I doubt it"? We may doubt the word of another because we question the motives of the one who speaks. That's appropriate, but to question the motives of every person who speaks to us destroys all possibility of meaningful human relationship.

We may doubt because what is affirmed doesn't fit into the framework of our previous experience. It is proper to try to fit all that we confront into a coherent pattern, but we cannot limit the range of possibilities to our present perception of the way things are. Or we may doubt because no "proof" is offered for the claims that are made. Again, it is appropriate to ask for evidence, but finally life is a mystery that is beyond proof. Within narrow and restricted ranges of experience, we can ask for proof, but when we get to the genuinely significant questions of human existence, we live by faith.

Granted that the incident in which Jesus and Peter walked on the water does not fit easily into our experience of the world. Granted that we have no proof that such a thing happened. But we need to try to understand what is being affirmed through this dramatic account before we let our doubts cause us to dismiss the story as nonsense. Peter saw Jesus walking on the water and cried out to him, "Lord, if it is you, bid me come to you on the water." When Jesus told him to come on, "Peter got out of the boat and walked on the water and came to Jesus; but when he saw the wind, he was afraid, and beginning to sink he cried out, 'Lord, save me.' Jesus immediately reached out his hand and caught him, saying to him, 'O man of little faith, why did you doubt?'" (vs. 29-31). Peter suddenly was panicked by his doubts. The incident helps us to see something of the nature and results of our doubts.

Jesus asked Peter, "Why did you doubt?" As we look more closely at what Peter did, we can begin to discern some of the things which may have led to his doubting at a crucial moment. Why did Peter doubt? Perhaps because he leaped into an experience mostly as a way of testing Jesus. "Lord, if it is you, bid me come to you on the water." Some of the disciples had earlier said that the figure they saw walking on the water was a ghost, but Peter decided to test Jesus in a radical way. There doesn't seem to have been much point in Peter walking on the water except to get some proof about who it was out there.

Speaking through the prophet Micah, God took issue with the faithlessness of the people in these terms. "For the Lord has a controversy with his people, and he will contend with Israel. 'O my people, what have I done to you? In what have I wearied you? Answer me! For I brought you up from the land of Egypt, and redeemed you from the house of bondage; and I sent before you Moses, Aaron, and Miriam . . . that you may know the saving acts of the Lord'" (Micah 6:2-5). God pointed the people of Israel to all of the evidence that they had been cared for. God had saved them from their slavery and sent great people to lead them. They could see the saving acts of the Lord. What more did they need to assure them of God's care for them?

Why did Peter doubt? Perhaps because he ventured out impulsively beyond the range of experience where he was capable of believing. Peter was ready to trust his Lord and to follow him, but Peter wasn't ready for the risks and threats of walking on the deep waters of the sea. We grow and mature in our faith, and when we venture too far beyond the point to which we have grown, we are vulnerable to disasterous doubt. We live with the assurance that God will bring us to a faith adequate for the life God intends for us.

Why did Peter doubt? Perhaps because he left the boat to go out on his own. For the early Christians, the boat was a symbol for the church, for the community of faith. Peter leaped out into the sea all by himself, and doubts engulfed him. He separated himself from the others, and when he found himself alone in the midst of the storm, the doubts assailed him. Our life of faith is nurtured and sustained when we are part of the community, the church. It is difficult to be an isolated Christian. It is hard to keep the faith when we separate ourselves from the fellowship of believers. Our faith is nurtured when we come together to pray for ourselves, for each other, for our world. Our faith is strengthened when we sing together of God's love and grace. Our faith is deepened when we witness the faith of others. When all of us together share our faith, the faith of each of us is strengthened.

Why did Peter doubt? Perhaps because he focused on the threats. "But when he saw the wind, he was afraid, and beginning to sink he cried out, 'Lord, save me.'" Peter became aware of all the threats in his situation, and panic struck, and he began to doubt, and he began to sink. We face threats and dangers. There is evil in our world that can hurt us and others. There is illness that can shatter us. There are disasters which can overtake us. It is right to take proper precautions in the face of such threats. But if our attention is focused on the threats, we miss the evidence of the loving, sustaining care of God. Preoccupation with the threats will cause the doubts to rise within us.

The question of Jesus to Peter confronts us: "Why did you doubt?" It is appropriate to bring a measure of doubt and skepticism into our world, and even into the religious dimensions of our lives. But the question of Jesus probes and exposes our failure to nurture the faith that can sustain and strengthen us. In his grace and mercy, God still makes known the divine presence, that we may believe and that we may know the saving acts of the Lord.

21

Should Not You Have Had Mercy?

The Question of Jesus
"Should not you have had mercy on your fellow servant, as I had mercy on you?" (Matt. 18:33).

We are constantly taking our temperature as a society. Many kind of thermometers are employed to assess the state of our health: the rate of inflation, the Dow-Jones industrial average, the amount of the money supply, the unemployment rate, the whole price index, the average family income, the amount of retail sales, the exchange rate of the dollar on foreign money exchanges, the suicide rate, the infant mortality rate, the number of TV sets per family, the balance of trade, the number of doctors per hundred thousand persons, the crime rate, the change in the crime rate. The list goes on endlessly. There seems no end to the statistics that can be accumulated about human activities.

It is not entirely clear that all of this temperature-taking is itself a sign of health. A healthy person doesn't have to get up every morning and take her temperature to find out how healthy she is. She just goes about the business of the day. A healthy institution isn't constantly assessing itself to find out how it is. It just goes on about its business. To be sure, there need to be health checkups for people and assessments for institutions of where they are and where they are going. Some statistics are helpful in making such assessments and in planning for the future, and the compilation of statistics certainly provides employment for a good number of economists, statisticians, and computer programmers.

Behind all the figures and measurement, behind all the thermometer readings and check-ups, there is a fundamental question—What is health? What is a healthy society? What is a healthy institution? What is a healthy relationship? Who is a healthy person? These turn out to be rather difficult questions, and the search for answers turns out to be an elusive quest. Perhaps we know what a healthy body is, even though that may not be as precise in definition as first appears. A healthy body is one that functions well, in which all of the organs do well what they are designed to do, in which the organism as a whole has balance and vitality. But who is a healthy person? Is it one who can relate and share feelings, or one who has an inner core of privacy? Is it one who can cope with every circumstance with confidence, or one who is well aware that life is finally not controllable? Is it one who lives without fear or anxiety, or one who is sensitive to the threats which imperil life on this earth? Is it one who makes commitments which lead to intense involvement, or one who remains cool and aloof with no risk of fanaticism? People have different definitions of health and put different interpretations on the meaning of health. Behavior that one person would view as healthy would be seen by another as rigid. Attitudes that one person would view as positive would be seen by another as compulsive. Style that would be seen by one person as creative would be seen by another as irresponsible. There is no absolute standard to determine the health of a person.

What is a healthy society? One that provides for the physical needs of its members from the day of birth to the day of death? One that can give the security of being able to destroy any enemy who might pose a threat? One that attains a certain level of artistic and cultural sophistication? One that is constantly expanding its wealth and productivity? One which allows the fullest possible participation of all of its members in the process of governing? One that provides the conditions in which each member can reach his or her fullest potential? There are many ways to talk about and seek to measure the health of a society.

Jesus told a story that suggests another measure to check the health of a person or a society, a measure that is frequently not applied to an individual or a community. It is the story of the servant who owed an enormous debt to the king, a debt so big that even in a time of million dollar salaries, it staggers the imagination. The servant couldn't pay, and the king ordered him to be sold, along with his wife and children. In panic the servant pleaded with the king to be patient for a time and promised that he would pay the debt. The king took pity on the servant. He didn't just give him more time to repay the debt but cancelled the debt altogether. By his action, the king expressed a remarkable sensitivity to the plight of the servant and his family, and a truly unusual capacity for pity.

As the story proceeds, the focus shifts from the king to the servant, who has been so marvelously freed from the awful threat of being sold into slavery, along with his wife and children. We can have some sense of what the servant must have felt when he heard that not only was the prospect of being sold into slavery removed but that he didn't have to spend all of his energy and resources in repaying what he owed. He must have been in a state of euphoria as he left the king's presence. But as he went out, he met another servant who owed him a small amount, twenty dollars or so. He grabbed the other servant by the throat and demanded that he pay the debt immediately. The man said that he couldn't pay it right now and pleaded with him to be patient and give a little more time. But the first servant refused and had the one who owed him thrown into prison until the debt could be repaid.

Other servants saw what happened. They knew how much the king had done for this man, and they were greatly distressed that the one who had had such pity shown toward him should show so little pity toward another. So they went and told the king, who reacted with anger. The king called back the servant to whom he had forgiven so much and blasted him, "You wicked servant! I forgave you all that debt because you besought me; and should not you have had mercy on your fellow servant, as I had mercy on you?" (Matt. 18:32f.).

Should not you have had mercy? The servant who was forgiven so much and yet refused to forgive another so little was a sick man. His behavior was totally deficient in every mark of humanity. We find the king justified in his anger toward a man who would act as this man did. The story and the question point to another measure of health. A healthy person is one able to show mercy. It is a mark of health to show mercy toward those who have wronged us in some way. It is a mark of health to show mercy toward those who are weaker than we are. It is a mark of health to show mercy toward those in need.

In spite of our instinctive reaction to the story of Jesus, we must acknowledge that the answer to the question, "Should not you have had mercy?" does not come easily. We do not always think of health and strength as being defined by the capacity for mercy. A healthy, strong person—one who won't let people trample over his rights and who takes care of those who try, or one who can transcend the hurts which others do to offer mercy? A healthy, strong person—one who fights her way to equal standing with the powerful, or one who has the capacity to think about the needs of the weak? A healthy, strong person—one who uses the resources of life to provide for himself, or one who offers help to those who need it?

Should not you have had mercy? Health is not found in the ability to get even. Health is not found in the ability to overpower others. Health is not found in the ability to exploit others. The servant of the king was a sick man. One measure of health is our ability to show mercy.

The measure of mercy can also help in checking the health of a community or a society. There is justice in people having to earn what they get. This world is not set up for a free lunch. Persons must work, for that is the only way they will survive on this planet. A healthy society provides people the opportunity to work, but the truly healthy society finds the ways to be merciful to those who can't work. A healthy society nurtures the children who are not the productive members of the community. We have to ask what it says about the health of our society when we exploit children with violence, when we make them greedy by dangling goodies before them, when we make education a prime target for budget cuts. A healthy society cares for its weak and helpless. Welfare to those who can't work is not a drain on our resources but an evidence of our strength. A healthy society provides for the elderly when they are no longer the big consumers or the fashion setters. There is profound sickness in a society which says to any of its members that one is too old or too useless to be of value to our common life.

"Should not you have had mercy?" To show mercy is a sign of health. The achievement of health by any measure demands effort and concentration and discipline. Health is no easy achievement by any standard, and certainly not by the standard of the practice of mercy. It is often difficult to show mercy. A newspaper report recounted the reaction of a woman whose husband was killed by a fourteen-year-old neighbor. When the boy was brought to trial, he was sentenced as a juvenile instead of being sent to the Superior Court, and was given an extended period in a psychiatric hospital in an effort to rehabilitate him. The woman was angry at the way in which the boy was treated. "I'm stunned . . . something like this wouldn't happen in any other country." We can understand the woman's reaction. Her husband was killed. The one who killed him appeared to her not to be punished adequately. We can understand such a reaction, but must say that there is no health in the desire to destroy the one who wronged her. To show mercy to the guilty is not easy. To show mercy to the weak is not easy.

The story of Jesus, and the question in that story, helps us to find the hard way to health through mercy. For the story sets into perspective the response called for by the question of Jesus that we should have mercy. Why should we have mercy on others? Because when we are called to show mercy to others, it is as those to whom mercy has been shown. We don't want to push too hard the line that every person should get exactly what he or she deserves, for we don't want all that we deserve. The point of the parable is the overwhelming mercy of the king contrasted with the little expected of the servant. The king was owed an enormous amount, but he didn't just grant the request of the servant for more time; he cancelled the whole debt. The servant who owed his fellow servant a very small amount also asked for more time, but even that was refused.

We live daily by the mercy of God, a mercy which bears with our transgressions, a mercy that sets aside what we owe to God, a mercy that cares for us in our weakness, a mercy which reaches out to our need. That is the context of the question of Jesus to us, "Should not you have had mercy?" We are to have mercy because mercy has been shown to us. Jesus makes clear application of the story. When the king heard what the servant to whom he had shown such mercy had done to his fellow servant, he got angry and "delivered him to the jailers, till he should pay all his debt." And the application of Jesus. "So also my heavenly Father will do to every one of you, if you do not forgive your brother from your heart" (v. 35).

Should you not have had mercy? Mercy is a sign of health, for God has shown mercy toward us and has made us creatures who can be merciful to one another. In another word of Jesus: "Blessed are the merciful, for they shall obtain mercy."

22

Who Did the Will of His Father?

The Question of Jesus
"Which of the two did the will of his father?" (Matt. 21:31).

Seminary deans get a good deal of esoteric mail. One seminary regularly got letters signed "Jesus Christ," which had all kinds of advice about what young ministers should be taught. Another regular correspondent was faithful in reporting the lastest signs that the world was coming to an end, probably within the next twenty-four to forty-eight hours. Then there were the letters from the man who insisted that it was the will of God that he be on the seminary faculty.

There are some difficulties in the notion of the will of God. First, there is the issue of exactly what we mean when we talk about the will of God for us. Does it mean that God has a blueprint for our lives? To use a metaphor such as blueprint suggests that there is a plan for everything we do. When something happens, people often say that it was the will of God, with the implication that God is in charge of everything that happens in our world, down to the smallest detail in the life of every person. The view that God's will is expressed in everything that happens can be pressed on to a position that God has ordained from the beginning of time all that has happened, is happening, and ever will happen. It's all in the mind of God from eternity.

Such understanding of the will of God raises issues related to the conviction that human beings are free and responsible persons. The doctrine of predestination has never been easy to relate

136

to the doctrine of human responsibility. If it is God's will that makes something happen, do the decisions we make have any significance? It feels to us as though we have real options, real choices to make. How often we struggle in anguish with a decision. All of our struggle seems to be an illusion or a a cruel joke if God has determined all the time what was going to happen, if God knew what was going to happen from the beginning. Beyond such theoretical difficulties, does it make any difference to relate what we do and the decisions we make to some notion of the will of God for us, or do we function just as well without any reference to what God might want?

Second, there is the difficulty that even if we figure out how to talk in a meaningful way about the relation between God's ordaining will and our responsible freedom, how do we know what God's will is for us? If God wants something of us, precisely what? We can talk in abstraction about God's will and what God wants, and we can make various suggestions about how we might come to know God's will through reading the Bible or prayer or a word directly from the Lord. But when we get up against specific decisions of real life, there is often little clarity about what God's will is in that situation. Should I or should I not take the new job that will further my career and provide everything for my family except my presence for long periods? How shall I respond when my children want something that seems important to them and their peers, but which raises questions of standards and values for me? How long shall I continue a relationship with a person to whom I have some responsibility but that is becoming a destructive situation involving burdens beyond my bearing? Should I or should I not marry this person?

Most often we are faced with situations where the decisions are not clear-cut, clean, or unambiguous. We have to weigh conflicting values. When we do one thing, we are unable to do another thing that has a legitimate claim also on our time and attention. We are genuinely perplexed not only about what is the right thing to do but even what it is we want to do. We can talk about the will of God, but how often do we get down to making the real decisions of life and there seems to be no clear word from the Lord.

Third, there is the difficulty that claims that to know God's will can lead to inappropriate and insensitive behavior. Absolute knowledge is never given to any human being, and to claim to have such knowledge is to claim too much. Absolute certainty about what the future will bring is never given to any person, and to claim such certainty is to claim too much. No matter how much discernment we gain into God's will for the world and for ourselves, we remain finite, limited, fallible human beings. A conviction about God's will has the risk of leading us to forget our human limitations.

To claim to know too much of the will of God can foster some unattractive human qualities. A sense of arrogance can tempt those who believe that they have a superior understanding of God, or a special gift of God's revelation. Those who are too sure about what God wants may be driven to the destruction of significant human relationships and values. To be too sure of what we know may lead us to pay insufficient attention to what others know or perceive. The line between meaningful commitment and destructive fanaticism is a fine one.

Finally, there is the difficulty with some of the biblical imperatives delivered as the will of God. Did God really tell Abraham to take his son Isaac and offer him as a burnt offering? Granted, God stayed Abraham's hand at the last moment, but did God intend that a child should be bound and put on an altar and threatened with burning? Or is the biblical witness accurate when God tells Saul to smite the Amalekites and destroy every thing, slaying men and women and infants? Did God become angry when Saul failed to kill all those people?

How are we to hear the will of God in the words of Jesus when he said: "Go, sell what you have, and give to the poor" (Mark 10:21)? Or what is the will of God when Jesus said: "If any one comes to me and does not hate his own father and mother and wife and children and brothers and sisters, yes, and even his own life, he cannot be my disciple" (Luke 14:26)? Are those literal commands that speak to us exactly what God wants us to do? If not, what is the will of God being spoken through them, and how do we know what that will is?

Such difficulties with the concept of God's will give fair warning that it is a notion of some subtlety and complexity. Simplistic assertions that God wills this, or that, or the other thing need to be examined with considerable care. Yet it is fundamental to the Christian conviction about God and God's dealing with persons to talk about the will of God for us and for the world. Jesus' whole life manifested the sense that he was under the claims of God, and that he was responsible to express God's will in what he did and said. Particularly in the Gospel of John there is direct and explicit assertion that Jesus is on this earth to do the will of God. On one occasion the disciples urged Jesus to eat, and he said to them, "My food is to do the will of him who sent me, and to accomplish his work" (John 4:34). On another occasion his enemies were questioning his claims about his relationship to God, and Jesus said to them, "I can do nothing on my own authority; as I hear, I judge; and my judgment is just, because I seek not my own will but the will of him who sent me" (John 5:30). Then there was the dramatic scene in the Garden of Gethsemane when Jesus prayed that he might be spared from the suffering and death which he saw facing him. Jesus prayed for what he wanted but ended his prayer by surrendering himself to the will of God. "My Father, if this cannot pass unless I drink it, thy will be done" (Matt. 26:42). Throughout his life and ministry Jesus worked and spoke with the awareness that he was here to do the will of God and that God was indeed working that will through him.

Jesus taught us to pray to God, "Thy will be done, on earth as it is in heaven." We sometimes use impersonal and mechanistic metaphors in seeking to grasp what Jesus asks us to pray for. This leads to difficulties both for our understanding of God and for our interpretation of our own experience. To say that everything that happens does so because God has willed that specific event in some unchangeable order of events drawn up in eternity, leads to the assertion that the car skidding on a slick pavement and killing four teenagers is the will of God. There are ways of talking about how God exercises the divine will in our life that violates our sense that we make significant decisions and that we are rightly held accountable for what we do and say.

There is no simple formula that states precisely the relation between God's ordaining will and human responsible freedom. But there are ways of talking that may be more helpful than blueprint language or will-from-eternity language. For example, we might talk about God's having a purpose for our lives, a purpose that we can deny or fulfill by what we do, a purpose that God works out in and through and in spite of what we do. When we pray that God's will be done, we are praying that in what we do and in what happens in our world the intent of God for all of creation be fulfilled.

To be able to pray that God's will be done, to believe that somehow God's will can be worked out through our lives, to have the conviction that our lives can count in God's eternal purpose, makes a change in how we view ourselves. Such prayers and beliefs and convictions mean that life is not ours to do with entirely as we please. We can squander our lives and destroy our talents and waste our opportunities; but if we do that, it is of serious consequence, for God has a will and purpose for us. When we do not realize what we ought to be, we are denying not only ourselves but also what God intends. A conviction about the will of God gives seriousness and importance as we seek to fashion our lives. A conviction about the will of God gives us a standard by which to measure who we are and what we are doing. A conviction about the will of God makes possible genuine freedom. It might seem that freedom would come if we were autonomous creatures, responsible to no one but ourselves. But hard experience has demonstrated that we are vulnerable to the claims of many powers who would shape us and influence us and control us—the claim that we have to use the latest product, the claim that we must be approved by others, the claim that we have to move in the right social circles. If we do not seek the will of the one God, we will serve the wills of the many gods. The phrase from the collect puts it in sharp terms—we pray to the God "whose service is perfect freedom." When we seek the will of God, we are freed from the compulsive demands of the many powers who would shape our lives. One piece of good news of the Christian faith is that God does have a will for our lives and that we can seek to fulfill that will in who we are and how we live.

Jesus told a story about two sons, and at the end of the story he asked the question, "Which of the two did the will of his father." Granted that there is a will of God for this world and for the lives of others and for our own lives, can we ever know what that will is? Can we answer the question of Jesus about which person did the will of the Father? We have reflected earlier on the difficulty of knowing what God wants when we get down to specific cases. Can we ever be sure what God wills? In the store of Jesus, the father asked one son to go and work in the vineyard, and he replied that he would not do it, but afterward he was sorry for his words and went to work as his father had asked him. The father asked the other son also to work in the vineyard, and he said that he would, but then he did not go. Then the question: "Which of the two did the will of the father?" Those who heard him answered that the first son had done the will of the father.

We do not have absolute knowledge of the will of God, and must always declare what we believe to be that will with the humility of our human limitations. But as the parable of Jesus makes clear, it is possible in many circumstances to give a confident answer to the question of Jesus about which of the two did the will of his father. Here is a person who alienated those who wanted a close relationship; here is a person who found the strength to seek reconciliation with one who had violated a relationship. Which of the two . . . ? Here is a person who crippled another by destroying his confidence; here is a person who supported and sustained another. Which of the two . . . . Here is a person who tempted another to what was evil and destructive; here is a person who inspired another to be better than she was. Which of the two . . . ?

To affirm that there is a will of God for our lives, and that we can know it, will not solve all the ambiguities of life nor make all our decisions clear and simple. But we are not without knowledge of what God wills for us and for our world, for we can answer the question of Jesus: "Which of the two did the will of his father?"

23

Which Is Greater?

The Question of Jesus
"For which is greater, the gift or the altar that makes the gift sacred?" (Matt. 23:19).

Students seeking letters of recommendation from faculty members are asked to sign a request form, and to indicate whether the letter is to be confidential or whether the student is to have access to it. The form poses a dilemma. On the one hand, students would like to know what the faculty members say about them. On the other hand, they figure that the letter carries more weight if the reader knows that the person about whom it is written will not see it. For there is the suspicion, probably well founded, that people writing comments about another will not be as honest or critical if they know that the person will see it.

Sometimes it seems that Christians have particular difficulty in making negative judgments, and in making them directly to the person. Members of a seminary admissions committee have reported that the recommendations for applicants which come from ministers tend to be extraordinarily effusive and uniformly positive and that such recommendations are frequently discounted heavily. Christians want to be loving, and it seems unloving to confront people with their faults and failures. Christians are concerned about their relationships with others, and fearful that honest rebuke of another will harm the good feeling between them. Christians tend to see and to stress the good in others, for they believe in the goodness that God has created in all persons. Christians are aware of their own limitations and are therefore reluctant to confront others with their failures lest they sound self-righteous.

Yet it is strange that Christians have hang-ups about confronting people when there are disagreements to be settled or faults to be noted. It is clear that Jesus was willing to speak the critical word with impressive boldness. Repeatedly he spoke the hard, even brutal, word to the scribes and the Pharisees. "Woe to you, scribes and Pharisees, hypocrites." That is not exactly the friendly opening gambit. He went on: "You also outwardly appear righteous to men, but within you are full of hypocrisy and iniquity" (Matt. 23:28). Whatever others may think of their outward appearance, Jesus was not taken in by it and was quite willing to let them know. At one point he broke out in sharp language of condemnation as he addressed them: "You serpents, you brood of vipers, how are you to escape being sentenced to hell?" (v.33). At yet another point, he charged them with being unable to see what was going on. "Woe to you, blind guides." "You blind men." "You blind fools." Jesus was clear that the scribes and Pharisees were wrong, that they didn't know what was going on, and he was bold to tell them so. There was no hesitation on the part of Jesus to confront those he believed were in serious error.

What brought forth such harsh judgment about the blindness of the Pharisees? "Woe to you, blind guides, who say, 'If any one swears by the temple, it is nothing; but if any one swears by the gold of the temple, he is bound by his oath.' You blind fools! . . . And you say, 'If any one swears by the altar, it is nothing; but if any one swears by the gift that is on the altar, he is bound by his oath.' You blind men!" (Matt. 23:16-19). Jesus is clear that the scribes and Pharisees were not seeing clearly, as he calls them blind guides and blind fools and blind men. What is it that they were missing? What is going on here? Why is Jesus so vehement in his denunciation of them? Apparently there is a controversy about how binding are the oaths which people swear. Oaths were taken seriously. Oaths had a binding power. But there was some gradation in the seriousness with which oaths must be taken. So the scribes and Pharisses say that if any one swears by the temple, that oath doesn't count; but if he swears by the gold in the temple, then the oath is binding. They say that if anyone swears by the altar, the oath has no power; but if he swears by the gift on the altar, then the oath is binding.

Jesus says that the distinctions that the scribes and Pharisees are making about oaths are wrong, but why is Jesus so vehement in his attack on them? The temple and the altar are representative of the presence of God; they are the holy and sacred places. The gold of the temple and the gift on the altar are visible, tangible objects; they are the "real things" that can be touched and sold and traded and hoarded. Jesus calls them blind guides and blind men and blind fools, and he asks the question: "For which is greater, the gold or the temple that has made the gold sacred? . . . For which is greater, the gift or the altar that makes the gift sacred?" (vs. 17, 19).

For which is greater? Jesus calls them blind. They are blind because they discern only the physical, material objects. They see the gold and they see the gifts, but they fail to perceive the reality of the God who makes the gold valuable and the gifts meaningful. They have eyes that can see the physical world, but they lack the ability to discern the world of the Spirit. They can see the objects of this world, but Jesus calls them blind because they cannot see through the objects to the realm of the sacred and the divine. Which is greater, the gold or that which makes the gold sacred; the gift or that which makes the gift sacred? They are blind to the matters of greater import.

Jesus calls them fools. They are fools because they put more value on that which is of lesser worth, and lesser value on that which is of more worth. That is as good a definition of a fool as one can find. A fool is one who does not know the value of what is being dealt with, one who passes by the things of genuine worth to invest heavily in things that don't count that much. The question of Jesus is critical. Which is of more value? If the scribes and Pharisees don't know whether the gold or God, the gift or the divine, are of more value, they are fools! That is what Jesus calls them.

What has all of this to do with us? We don't go around swearing by gold or temples, by gifts or altars. Involved arguments about which oaths are more binding don't seem to have a great deal of urgency for us. While we use oaths in some situations, the oath does not have the aura or power it had in Jesus' day. This talk of swearing by the temple or swearing by the gold sounds strange to us. But the issue that Jesus presses with his question to the scribes and Pharisees confronts us. The issue presses us in a different way but just as urgently. For which is greater?

We, too, are subject to the blindness that restricts the "real world" to the world we can see and touch and handle. We deal readily with the objects that have a solidity and certainty about them. The chair is real, for we can pick it up, paint it, sit on it, shove it in the corner, trip over it. The piece of bread is real, for we can cut it, toast it, butter it, eat it. The dog is real, for we can put him out, play with him, watch his tail wag, hear him bark. In our blindness we may believe that the world of the chair and the piece of bread and the dog is all there is. We fail to discern the world unseen to human eyes, the world of the Spirit, the world of the divine, the world of the holy. We have not looked at our world with the eyes of faith, which enable us to discern the presence of God. We have seen the gold but not the temple. We have seen the gift but not the altar.

We are tempted to put a higher value on the things of this world. We find our sense of worth in the things we have accumulated. We go to great lengths to protect our things. We struggle and fight in order to acquire more things. We devote our time, our thought, our energy to the getting of things. Things can become more important than time to reflect. Things can become more important than learning to enjoy them. Things can become more important than sustaining the bonds which bind our lives to others. The Pharisees valued the gold above the temple, the gift above the altar. Jesus calls them blind fools. For which is greater? The question of Jesus to the Pharisees and his brutal description of them must raise for us the question of whether we are being blind fools who do not discern the reality beneath the things and who value the things more than they are worth. "For which is greater, the gold or the temple that has made the gold sacred? . . . For which is greater, the gift or the altar that makes the gift sacred?"

Our faith as Christians gives a helpful perspective and insight as we are involved with the things of this world. First, the Christian affirmation about the nature of God's creation makes no denial of the reality or the importance of things. The gold is real; the gift on the altar is real. The chair, the piece of bread, the dog are real. We are physical creatures who live in a world of physical objects. We do not find the meaning or fulfillment of our lives by trying to rise above our physical natures into some spiritual, immaterial realm. The objects of our world are important. We are significantly affected by the physical surroundings in which we find ourselves. The shape and style of a building makes an impact on how we function and feel. Chairs and tables are signficant objects in our lives. Without physical food, we do not long endure in the life on this earth.

In our Christian conviction, we affirm this solid, material, physical world, not only that it is but that it is important. For at the center of our faith is a person, with a body like our bodies, with flesh like our flesh. Jesus shared fully in our experience on this earth, which means that he ate bread as we eat bread, that he dealt with the things of this world as we deal with the things of this world, that he had needs for his physical body as we have needs for our physical bodies.

A second perspective given by our faith is that things are not sacred in themselves. Things are real, but they are not the ultimate reality. Things have worth, but they are not of absolute value. Things have meaning, but they are not the source of all meaning. Things endure, but they are not eternal. Things are things; they are not God. The possessions we have are useful to us, but they do not give us worth, and if we seek to find our worth in what we possess, we distort both the things and ourselves. The possessions we have enrich our lives, but they do not provide the meaning of our existence, and if we seek to find meaning in the things, we are doomed to frivolity and disappointment. The possessions we have are valuable to us, but they do not define the purpose for which we live. If we live in order to acquire more and more, we have trivialized the life God has given to us.

The one who became flesh and dwelt among us shared our need for food and clothing and shelter, but Jesus did not devote his life to the acquisition of these things. Rather, when he had these things, he devoted his life to sharing with others, to ministering to others, to offering love and care to others, and to growing in his relationship with the God whom he called Father. Jesus had no uncertainty about which was greater, the gold or the temple, the gift or the altar.

A third perspective given by our faith is that things are gifts of God and are means by which we can discern the eternal and the divine. Jesus didn't condemn the gold in the temple or the gifts on the altar. He called the Pharisees blind fools because they didn't discern the holiness of God in the gold and the gifts. "For which is greater, the gold or the temple that has made the gold sacred? . . . For which is greater, the gift or the altar that makes the gift sacred?" In and beyond the things we touch and handle is the reality of the unseen. It is unseen, but it can be discerned in the things which are touched and handled. We have special places and special things that serve particularly to remind us of the power and the holiness and the presence of God. There was the gold in the temple and the gift on the altar for the Pharisees. Jesus affirmed the gold and the gift, and condemned the Pharisees for their blindness because they valued only the gold and the gift without letting them express the temple and the altar that made them sacred.

There are objects and places for us that have distinctive capacity to reflect the sacred. A church building is built of wood and stone and steel and concrete as every other building. A church building is furnished with carpet and furniture, and lighted with electricity. But because of what people have done there and continue to do there, the church is valued not for the building alone but because that place has peculiar capacity to enable people to discern God, and the goodness and power and love of God. As the people of faith gather about the table they know as the Lord's Table, they eat bread and drink wine, bread and wine that are part of the common stuff of life. But this bread and this wine have powerful potential to bring persons into a relationship with the God who came into this world in Jesus Christ.

As the people gather for worship, words are spoken, ordinary words spoken by ordinary people. In the same passage in which Jesus chastises the Pharisees for their blind foolishness, he talks about burdens, shoulders, fingers, deeds, honor, teachers, servants, sea, land, law, justice, mercy, cleansing, cup, plate, and on and on. They are all words used in the ordinary discourse of daily life, but the ordinary words used in worship are so shaped so that they may become to us the means through which God speaks. We are blind and foolish if we see only the building and eat only the bread and hear only the words but do not discern the God who makes the building and the bread and the words sacred.

It is not only the special places that help us to discern God. If we are not blind fools, all the food we eat speaks to us of the care and providence of God, the objects we handle make known to us the Creator of all that is. Through many human words and relationships, God expresses great love for us.

Jesus confronted the scribes and the Pharisees with a brutal but caring honesty, calling them blind fools who think that the gold in the temple and the gift on the altar, the things of this world, are the real things. "For which is greater," he asks, "the gold or the temple that has made the gold sacred?" "For which is greater," he asks, "the gift or the altar that makes the gift sacred?"

24

Would You Betray?

The Question of Jesus
"Judas, would you betray the Son of man with a kiss?" (Luke 22:48).

In her novel *The Severed Head*, Iris Murdoch assembles a cast of characters who are closely related to one another. The narrator is a middle-aged London business man. The other characters are the narrator's wife and brother and mistress, the wife's psychiatrist, and the pyschiatrist's sister. Only the imagination of a superb novelist could create the tangled relationships into which these people get themselves. The story opens as the narrator leaves his mistress. He returns home to his wife, who announces that she is leaving him for her psychiatrist. The narrator then falls in love with the psychiatrist's sister, only to be shattered when he catches the psychiatrist and sister in an incestuous relationship. The narrator's wife returns, and then his mistress and his brother decide to get married. But it turns out that his wife has been having an affair with his brother for years. After a few more convolutions, the mistress ends up with the psychiatrist, the wife ends up with the brother, and the narrator ends up with the psychiatrist's sister.

Just what is Iris Murdoch saying in such a bizarre and tangled story? That is not an easy question to answer, and no one can answer it fully and finally, but Murdoch is magnifying and dramatizing the reality of human betrayal. Every single character in the story violates a trust, not once but repeatedly. It is a caricature, and yet she uses the excesses of the story to give a sense of the pervasiveness of betrayal. She is saying that betrayal is an extensive if not a universal facet of human relationships. Furthermore, the betrayal is all done with a certain grace and flair. No character in the story is mean or ugly or nasty. They do not beat one another or flagrantly abuse one another. They are all sophisticated, attractive, concerned people. All of the betrayals are made under the guise of love. They do not set out to hurt one another. They do not hate one another. They believe they are acting from worthy motives and genuine concern. One other point to be noted in Murdoch's dramatization of betrayal is that the results are ambiguous but disasterous. Everyone is entangled in a web of emotional conflicts. They find themselves dealing with powerful forces that sweep them one way and then another. No character in the story finds sustained joy or satisfaction in any of the relationships.

The biblical stories of the ways in which people deal with one another confirm the pervasiveness of betrayal in human relationships. In the beginning, Cain violated the trust of a brother as he killed Abel. Twice, Jacob betrayed his brother Esau: He took advantage of Esau's hunger to take his birthright as elder son for a pottage of lentils, and he tricked their father Isaac into giving him the blessing that properly belonged to his brother. The brothers of Joseph betrayed him as they sold him into slavery in Egypt.

One of the poignant and dramatic stories of betrayal in the New Testament centers on Peter. Jesus had warned all of the disciples that they would fail him and leave him. Brash Peter had reacted briskly to that warning of Jesus with the confident assertion that even if all the others left him, he would never fall away. Then Jesus had told Peter that before the night was over he would deny him three times. As Jesus was in the Garden of Gethsemane that night, he was seized by soldiers and taken to the house of the high priest. Peter followed at a distance and moved into the courtyard of the high priest where a group was gathered around the fire. "Then a maid, seeing him as he sat in the light and gazing at him, said, 'This man also was with him.' But he denied it, saying, 'Woman, I do not know him.' And a little later someone else saw him and said, 'You also are one of them.' But Peter said, 'Man, I am not.' And after an interval of about an hour still another insisted, saying, 'Certainly this man also was with him; for he is a Galilean.' But Peter said, 'Man, I do not know what you are saying'" (Luke 22:56-60). Brash Peter, who had asserted so confidently that he would never leave Jesus, betrayed him as he denied repeatedly that he had ever been with Jesus or even known him. Jesus was right, of course, for not only Peter but all of the disciples deserted him.

There is a story of betrayal in the early Christian community. In those days the group of Christians shared everything in common, as people gave everything they owned to the community, and the community took care of the needs of all. A couple named Ananias and Sapphira joined the group, but they sold a piece of property and kept part of the proceeds for themselves. Peter could recognize betrayal when he saw it, and said to Ananias: "Why has Satan filled your heart to lie to the Holy Spirit and to keep back part of the proceeds of the land? While it remained unsold, did it not remain your own? And after it was sold, was it not at your disposal? How is it that you have contrived this deed in your heart? You have not lied to men but to God" (Acts 5:3f.). It wasn't just a matter of giving or not giving the money to the community. It was a matter of lying about what had been done, a betrayal of the trust which the people had to have in each other in order to survive.

The name above all names in the scripture identified with betrayal is Judas. Jesus was on the Mount of Olives with his disciples, where he had been praying that the bitter cup would be taken from him and that he would be spared the suffering and death. He came back from where he had gone alone to pray and found the disciples sleeping. He roused them and urged them to pray that they might not enter into temptation. "While he was speaking, there came a crowd, and the man called Judas, one of the twelve was leading them. He drew near to Jesus to kiss him; but Jesus said to him, 'Judas, would you betray the Son of man with a kiss?'" (Luke 22:47-48). It was particularly despicable that a disciple whom Jesus had selected and taught and ministered to would betray him, but even more heinous that he would betray him with a kiss. The kiss is an act of caring and bonding between two people, and to use that act to betray is a violent violation of trust.

"Would you betray the Son of man with a kiss?" Most of us would want to respond with an emphatic *no!* We would not be Judas and betray the Lord. We would not betray one another. But the perception of Iris Murdoch, and the behavior of the people in the biblical accounts, should make us cautious about too quick and facile an assertion that we would never be guilty of betrayal. When Peter declared so boldly that he would never deny Jesus, Matthew adds this word: "And so said all the disciples." They did not want to betray Jesus and yet they did. "Would you betray the Son of man with a kiss?" Lord, we hope not, but we are troubled by the betrayals of others and by the knowledge of our own frailty. We dare not answer the question of Jesus easily or casually.

As we confront the question of Jesus, it will help to explore why we cannot give an easy assurance that we will never betray him or others. Why do persons betray one another? Why do they violate the trust that has been put in them? Why do they bring the hurt and pain to another, which comes with a breaking of confidence? Why do they weaken the community, which is based on loyalty? Why do we betray one another? The novelist and the biblical writers alert us to some of the pressures and dynamics which lead persons to betrayal. First, we may betray others because we are afraid. Peter betrayed Jesus out of fear. Jesus had been seized by the authorities, and Peter feared what they would do to him if he acknowledged his relationship with Jesus.

It has often been fearful and costly business to be faithful to Jesus Christ. There have been martyrs who have paid the price of their faithfulness, but there have been others who did not find the courage or the strength and who in fear denied the Lord they would serve. We don't pronounce easy judgment on such people, for we have known the pressure of fear to betray him. Few of us have faced actual martyrdom, but few of us have escaped the failure to live out our commitment to Jesus. We are not ashamed of our Christian commitment but would just as soon not have it trumpeted about in this sophisticated crowd. We would like to take a stand for low-cost housing in our community but wonder what the reaction of our neighbors would be. We would like to be identified with Christ but hesitate because it doesn't quite fit the "macho" ideal of the peers whose opinion of us is important to us.

Our betrayal of Christ in fear is not only a denial of him but is also an abuse of the trust that others have put in us. Lillian Hellman described what it cost her to stand by friends who were under investigation during the McCarthy hysteria and notes that there were many others who were too afraid to pay the price she paid. Would you betray the Son of man? No, we would not, Lord, but we know the fear with which we must struggle if we are to keep faith with you.

Second, we may betray others and the Lord because of our

self-centeredness. The biblical story doesn't say why Ananias and Sapphira kept part of the proceeds of the sale of their land for themselves. They didn't have to give anything, but they couldn't quite bring themselves to give everything. Perhaps they had some things they wanted to do with their money. Perhaps they weren't quite sure that the community really could provide for them if they gave everything away. Whatever the reason, their own interest as they perceived it got in the way of their loyalty to the community and led them to betray the trust that others had put in them.

We can relate to Ananias and Sapphira, for we know that our actual or perceived self-interests are often in conflict with our loyalty and obligations to others. It becomes inconvenient to go to work in the soup kitchen on Thursday as we had promised, and so we don't go, leaving the staff short-handed. We would like to make a larger pledge to support the world mission of the church, but worry whether we will have saved enough to guarantee that we can do all the things we want to do when we retire. It is not easy to decide how our legitimate self-interests relate to the claims on our resources for service to others in Christ's name. Would you betray the Son of man? No, we would not, Lord, but we know how difficult it is to limit our self-centeredness as we struggle to keep faith with you.

Third, we may betray others and the Lord because we are greedy. More than self-interest may drive us as we seem to have some compulsive need to get more and more and more for ourselves. One of the motivations which seems to have moved Judas to betray Jesus was greed. He was paid good money for the betrayal. Succumbing to the temptation to abscond with funds, an employee betrays the trust placed in her or him, driven by the greedy desire for more money. But the greed that drives us to betray a trust doesn't have to issue an action as dramatic as absconding with big funds; it may be only a matter of fudging a bit on an expense account or taking a few stamps for personal letters. Would you betray the Son of man? No, we would not, Lord, but we know the greed in ourselves that makes it hard to keep faith with you.

Reasons for betrayal such as fear and self-interest and greed are fairly straightforward, and we have all struggled with them. Two other reasons for betrayal, which can be discerned in the scripture account of Ananias and Judas, are of a different order. The decision of Judas to betray Jesus is interpreted in this fashion:

"Then Satan entered into Judas called Iscariot" (Luke 22:3). When Peter saw what Ananias was doing in withholding part of the money, he said to him, "Ananias, why has Satan filled your heart to lie to the Holy Spirit and to keep back part of the proceeds of the land?"(Acts 5:3). Betrayal is the work of Satan within them and within us. Betrayal is a deep, pervasive corruption of the human spirit. To betray is to be in the grip of powers that move with compelling force in our lives. Betrayal is an expression of profound evil, evil as personified in the figure of Satan. When we betray the Lord and one another, we are giving expression to the deep sickness of spirit.

In the effort to understand the roots of betrayal, we note finally that Judas betrayed Jesus with a kiss, a manifestation of love and affection. The kiss as a way of pointing out Jesus to his enemies seems a particularly heinous act. Yet it is possible to interpret the act of Judas as a sincere expression of a strategy that he thought would push ahead the goals for which Jesus was striving. In this interpretation, Judas was impatient and wanted Jesus to seize authority. He thought that his arrest would force Jesus to exercise the power Judas believed he had and to establish his kingdom. No one can know what was in the mind of Judas, but it can be argued that he kissed Jesus in genuine conviction that what he was doing would further the cause to which Jesus and Judas were both committed. In this interpretation, the betrayal came out of love.

All of the characters in Iris Murdoch's novel believe that they are acting in love. As they move from one person to another, they have convinced themselves that they are doing it because they are drawn to the other in love, and that they have no choice but to go to the one they love. They even succeed in convincing themselves that what they are doing is best for the one they are leaving and betraying. The interpretation of the action of Judas and the description of the characters by Murdoch have an authentic ring, for we are aware that we betray others in love. We betray our relationship as spouse or parent or child or friend if love compels us to try to make decisions for them that only they ought to make, if love compels us to support them in ways that make them weaker rather than stronger, if love compels us to an impatience that will not allow them to work out their own way of coping with the challenges they confront. It is a sobering but true observation that even our love for another may lead to betrayal of the other.

The results of betrayal are disasterous. Peter wept bitterly when he spoke the third word of denial of his Lord. Judas destroyed himself when he confronted the outcome of what he had done. Peter spoke to Ananias about his betrayal. "When Ananias heard these words, he fell down and died." Peter spoke to Sapphira about her betrayal. "Immediately she fell down at his feet and died." The characters of Murdoch's story destroyed themselves and others. When one person betrays another, there is anguish and disillusion and a ruptured relationship.

We cannot answer with absolute confidence the question of Jesus: "Would you betray the Son of man with a kiss?" We can only know our danger and seek to prepare ourselves for the testing of our loyalty, which will come. And we can hear the word of Jesus to his disciples as he knew what was facing him and them on the night of his arrest. "Pray that you may not enter into temptation" (Luke 22:40).

25

Why Are You Troubled?

The Question of Jesus
"Why are you troubled, and why do questionings rise in your hearts?" (Luke 24:38).

Part of the process of dealing with other people is trying to figure out how they will react in certain situations. Sometimes we are right on target; sometimes we miss badly. For example, we make some special effort to do something nice for someone: We bring home a bell for a friend we know collects bells; we go out of our way to deliver some papers we think are important to a colleague; we make a special effort on a Sunday afternoon to call on a friend who doesn't get out much any more. We do such things because we anticipate that people will be pleased and appreciative. Frequently they are, but sometimes we are fooled. Our effort is met with massive indifference; they just don't seem to care that we brought them a gift or delivered the papers or made the call. Or there is a sense of suspicion, as though they wonder what we want from them, what kind of ulterior motive is at work in us.

The disciples and followers of Jesus suffered a tragic and catastrophic loss that brought an end to their hopes and dreams and aspirations. Many had left everything to follow Jesus in the expectation that he was going to bring a new order into their world, that we was going to deal with the oppression under which they suffered, that he was going to lead them into a new kingdom. All that hope was shattered when Jesus was executed on a cross. Luke describes two of Jesus' followers as they made their weary way back home from Jerusalem after the crucifixion: "And they stood still, looking sad" (Luke 24:17).

What kind of reaction might be expected if the miracle happened and Jesus came back to his followers? What kind of reaction would seem to come out of an experience of meeting Jesus and knowing that he was alive? One would anticipate that there would be wonder and excitement. If the death of Jesus brought despair, surely the resurrection of Jesus will bring hope. If the death of Jesus brought sorrow, surely the resurrection of Jesus will bring joy. As the Gospels record the events of the first Easter, there is wonder and excitement and hope and joy. Jesus met the two followers who were leaving Jerusalem to go back home to Emmaus, the two whom Luke describes as looking sad. As they walked along, Jesus talked with them, but they didn't recognize him. When they came to the village where they were headed, the two men invited Jesus in to spend the night. As they ate together, Jesus broke the bread and gave it to them. Through that act, their eyes were opened and they recognized him. At that point they said to one another: "Did not our hearts burn within us while he talked to us on the road?" They raced back to Jerusalem to tell the others the good news that Jesus had walked with them and broken bread with them. They were two excited and happy men.

But that was not the universal reaction. For as the two men were telling their story to the others, "Jesus himself stood among them. But they were startled and frightened, and supposed that they saw a spirit. And he said to them, 'Why are you troubled, and why do questionings arise in your hearts?'" (Luke 24:36-38). A picture of the first Easter Day as a day of unbounded joy and excitement and faith and celebration might be the picture we would expect, but it is not the picture the Gospels paint. There was doubt that day. There was fear. There were questionings. There were troubled people, so that Jesus even had to ask his disciples: "Why are you troubled, and why do questionings rise in your hearts?"

As we contemplate the resurrection of Jesus Christ, there is the expected response from us. We rejoice that Jesus who came into our world bringing the love of God and manifesting the power of God was not destroyed by the powers of evil who killed him. We give thanks that we follow not just the teachings of a wise man who once lived but that we share our life journey with an ever-present Lord. We take hope in a life eternal from his triumph over his death on the cross. With good reason, Easter is the climax of the Christian year, a day of great affirmation, a day of lively celebration, a day of profound joy. But even as we give this expected response to the affirmation of the resurrection of our Lord, the question of Jesus to the disciples on that first Easter Day has point for many of us. "Why are you troubled?" If unbounded enthusiasm and unquestioning conviction are called for in response to the event celebrated on Easter, many of us don't make it. If Jesus asks us, "Why are you troubled, and why do questionings rise in your hearts?" we can respond to that.

First, we are troubled because it smacks of an unlikely occurrence for a man to be raised from the dead and to appear in the midst of his followers. John Train has collected a host of strange coincidences, weird statistics, bizarre situations in a book on remarkable occurrences, occurrences such as the collision in 1885 of the only two cars in the whole state of Ohio, the landing unhurt in eighteen inches of snow of an English airman blown from a bomber at 18,000 feet, the sentencing to jail of an eighty-two-year-old man for strangling his seventy-six-year-old wife after he had accused her of adultery. In some ways a resurrection strikes us as such an unlikely occurrence, and we are pushed to question whether such a thing really happened.

Was it all a hoax? Was it mass delusion? Was it a clever scheme to rally the scattered followers of Jesus? Was it wishful thinking? If we believe in a resurrection of a man from the dead, are we being naive and foolish? Why are you troubled? The disciples had trouble believing even when they encountered the risen Lord. They weren't quite sure about what they were seeing. "There were startled and frightened, and supposed that they saw a spirit."

Second, we are troubled not only because it seems an unlikely occurrence but because we are confronted with an event and a community and a claim that shatter our usual categories of interpreting our world and our lives. To affirm the resurrection of Jesus Christ moves us to a profoundly different way of dealing with our world and its problems. Denis Goulet in his book *The Uncertain Promise* writes of the ways in which technology shapes our world and our perceptions of it. "Technology cherishes rationality as a major value; to be rational is to view every experience as a problem which can be broken down into parts, reassembled, manipulated in practical ways, and measured in its effects . . . verifiability has supplanted truth."[10]

But the affirmation of the resurrection of Jesus Christ exposes us to a range of truth beyond rationality and verifiability, and that is troubling to us who are part of a technological time. The resurrection confronts us with a God who deals with evil and hate and death, not by rational solutions, not by breaking all experiences down into parts and putting them back together again. The cross manifested evil and hate and death in their most virulent and frightening form. There is a "rational" way to try to deal with these realities: Evil is controlled by vengeance and punishment; hatred is confronted with bigger walls and better protection; death is countered by building healthier bodies and refusing to accept it.

God's solution is beyond rationality and verifiability, for God's solution comes in the love, the grace, the mercy embodied in Jesus Christ, who lived and died and was raised from death. The fundamental issues and problems of life are finally beyond understanding and verifying; they are not problems to be solved but are to be coped with in such fashion that life can be carried on fully and faithfully. Life is set not in a context of technical structures but in the context of the essential hiddenness of reality, a reality that breaks through in events that communicate their meaning in ways beyond rational explanation. Such an event is the resurrection of Jesus Christ. All of this is troubling for us who like our world neat and orderly and rational. When Jesus asks why we are troubled, we respond that by his resurrection he has opened to us a world which is wonderful in its promise but frightening. It takes us beyond the safe realms where we can pretend that we understand and control.

Finally, we are troubled because in the risen Lord we are confronting the power and the love of God. The disciples were startled and troubled because they confronted a risen Lord, manifesting a power beyond that which they had seen before, even in the Jesus who had talked with such authority and healed with such compassion and stilled the waves with such quiet ease. The resurrection was and is God breaking into our world in a new way, and confronting such extraordinary manifestations of God is troubling. The experience of an Isaiah is well beyond the range of experience of most people, but the response of Isaiah to his confrontation with God is shared by all of us. Isaiah saw the Lord sitting upon a throne, high and lifted up. Isaiah's response was not jubliant delight that he had been give such a special revelation of God. Isaiah's response was not calm assurance that he could now be at ease because he had penetrated to the heart of the mystery of God. Rather, when Isaiah saw the Lord high and lifted up, he cried out, "Woe is me! For I am lost; for I am a man of unclean lips, and I dwell in the midst of a people of unclean lips; for my eyes have seen the King, the Lord of hosts!" (Isa. 6:5).

God's action is always wondrous and shattering, comforting and disturbing. "Why are you troubled, and why do questionings rise in your hearts?" We can understand how the disciples felt as they confronted the awesome manifestation of the power of God in the risen Christ, and must have sensed even in that moment that life would never again be the same for them. We can understand how Isaiah felt when he saw the Lord. In every instance when God confronts persons there are profound changes, and change is always troubling. As the risen Christ appeared to his disciples, he transformed their lives, he made new claim upon them, he set a new way before them. They would not go back to their homes to pick up an old life, but would be drawn together into a new community to make a new witness. The risen Christ transformed their lives, and he transforms our lives so that we are drawn together into a community of faith and seek to make a witness for Jesus Christ in our world.

Woody Allen once asked, "Do I believe in God?" His response to his own question: "I did until Mother's accident. She fell on some meat loaf, and it penetrated her spleen. She lay in a coma for months, unable to do anything but sing 'Granada' to an imaginary herring. Why was this woman in the prime of life so afflicted—because in her youth she dared to defy convention and get married with a brown paper bag on her head? And how can I believe in God when just last week I got my tongue caught in the roller of an electric typewriter? I am plagued by doubts. What if everything is an illusion and nothing exists? In that case, I definitely overpaid for my carpet. If only God would give me some clear sign."

But Woody Allen is a sufficiently penetrating theologian to know that God's signs don't come that clearly, and that when they do come they are not comforting but troubling. But there is a sign for us, a strong and powerful conviction that the crucified Lord returned to his people, a conviction that "the Lord has risen indeed." It is a disturbing world and a troubling world. But it opens to us the mystery and the wonder of this life, and opens for us a new way into communion with the God who loves us.

Notes

1. Thomas S. Kepler, *Jesus' Spiritual Journey—and Ours*. World Publishing Company, 1952, p. 91.

2. Clifton Fadiman, *Party of One*. World Publishing Company, 1955.

3. George Bernard Shaw, *Saint Joan*. Brentano's, 1924, p. 86.

4. James Dalton, ed., *Masterpieces of Religious Verse*. Harper & Row, 1948, p. 128.

5. Edith Wharton, *House of Mirth*. Scribner's, 1905, p. 315.

6. Gilbert Keith Chesterton, "O God of Earth and Altar, 1936." (Oxford University Press).

7. Chester Pennington, *God Has a Communication Problem*. Hawthorn Books, 1976, p. 3.

8. Alan Paton, *Cry, the Beloved Country*. Scribner's, 1948, p. 62.

9. Norman Cousins, *Anatomy of an Illness*. Norton, 1979.

10. Denis Goulet, *The Uncertain Promise*. IDOC/North America, 1977, p. 245.